Wynyard of High Wynyard. A novel of the present day. VOL. I

Charles Durant

The BiblioLife Network

This project was made possible in part by the BiblioLife Network (BLN), a project aimed at addressing some of the huge challenges facing book preservationists around the world. The BLN includes libraries, library networks, archives, subject matter experts, online communities and library service providers. We believe every book ever published should be available as a high-quality print reproduction; printed on- demand anywhere in the world. This insures the ongoing accessibility of the content and helps generate sustainable revenue for the libraries and organizations that work to preserve these important materials.

The following book is in the "public domain" and represents an authentic reproduction of the text as printed by the original publisher. While we have attempted to accurately maintain the integrity of the original work, there are sometimes problems with the original book or micro-film from which the books were digitized. This can result in minor errors in reproduction. Possible imperfections include missing and blurred pages, poor pictures, markings and other reproduction issues beyond our control. Because this work is culturally important, we have made it available as part of our commitment to protecting, preserving, and promoting the world's literature.

GUIDE TO FOLD-OUTS, MAPS and OVERSIZED IMAGES

In an online database, page images do not need to conform to the size restrictions found in a printed book. When converting these images back into a printed bound book, the page sizes are standardized in ways that maintain the detail of the original. For large images, such as fold-out maps, the original page image is split into two or more pages.

Guidelines used to determine the split of oversize pages:

• Some images are split vertically; large images require vertical and horizontal splits.
• For horizontal splits, the content is split left to right.
• For vertical splits, the content is split from top to bottom.
• For both vertical and horizontal splits, the image is processed from top left to bottom right.

WYNYARD OF HIGH WYNYARD.

WYNYARD OF HIGH WYNYARD.

A Novel of the Present Day.

BY

CHARLES DURANT.

"All's well that ends well."
SHAKESPEARE.

IN TWO VOLUMES.

VOL. I.

LONDON:
CHAPMAN & HALL, 193, PICCADILLY.

1878.

To
H. M. S.

CONTENTS OF VOL. I.

WYNYARD OF HIGH WYNYARD.

CHAPTER I.

FLOREAT ETONA.

" Ye distant spires, ye antique towers,
 That crown the wat'ry glade
Where grateful science still adores
 Her Henry's holy shade."
GRAY's Ode on Eton College.

A WARM, lovely evening in June; not a breath
of air moves the branches of the trees, and
the old college of Eton looks at her best.

The setting sun lights up the quaint dia-
mond-paned windows of the ancient build-
ings abutting on the quadrangle known as
" school yard," and the shadows are gradually lengthening around the fine old chapel.
Near one of the entrances the venerable

head master (in his younger days accounted one of the handsomest men of the age), attired in cap and gown, is calling over the names of the upper boys of the college. These, standing some twenty or thirty yards distant, raise their hats and call out, "Here, sir!" as their names are read over; a "præpositor," whose duty it is to note down any absentee, standing bareheaded. meanwhile by the side of the head master.

After "absence," as this ceremony is called, the boys still lingered about the quadrangle, breaking up into groups of three and four, and it was evident that the majority were discussing eagerly some event of more than passing importance. A few strolled over to the low wall facing two of the tutors' houses, where "Joby," the time-honoured bun-and-jam man, held his small court at intervals during the day; and these proceeded to discuss with gusto that dele-terious compound, conversing affably with Joby the while, and chaffing him about the new straw hat, with resplendent ribbon of palest blue, which that worthy had donned for the occasion—a special one, we may be sure.

A great cricket match had been decided that day on "Upper Club." The Eton eleven had played their annual match with Winchester, and the college founded by William of Wykeham had been vanquished by the superior play of their older rival, despite the gallant efforts of the Wykehamist captain, who, if he could not command success, determined at least to deserve it.

The form of Eton with the willow had been so good that the two reverend gentlemen, Mr. Satchell and Mr. George, who coached the eleven, regarded the issue of the match as a most satisfactory trial of Eton prowess; and, having deigned to communicate their august opinions to some of the sixth form, these latter had quoted the mighty augurs to other boys, and hopes now ran still higher in the school as to the probable result of the Harrow match, the greatest event in the year, and eagerly

looked forward to all through the mid-summer half. Indeed, the question as to who should be worthy to occupy the vacant places in the eleven was of far more importance than a change of head masters in the school, or in the ministry of the day. Some youthful Solons in the school, however, did not altogether eschew politics, and it was amusing enough to hear embryo statesmen of seventeen gravely discussing in "Pop"—as this miniature club and parliament was yclept—whether the conduct of the Government, in regard to some measure of reform, was not open to censure.

Nor did they confine their attention to the backslidings of the present age alone. Oliver Cromwell, Louis the Well-beloved, Charles I., and hosts of living and dead celebrities have had to stand in the pillory of Eton "Pop," and would no doubt have been startled could they have heard some of the charges preferred against them. Facts perhaps not always strictly historical; but then, in the heat of debate, surely older and

wiser heads than these are occasionally in-
accurate, and right honourable senators in a
higher assembly have been known to err on
the side of fiction.

To be a member of " Pop " at Eton was a
great proof of popularity, and occasionally
some captious critic (possibly envious of the
distinction himself) would complain that insufficient tribute was paid to the goddess of
Wisdom in this temple of sages—that pre-
ference was given to the successful cricketer,
the stalwart oar, the youth cunning at
"pepper-box," at "fives"—and a wail would
go up in the *Eton Chronicle* of " Cedant
arma togæ."   Then would a member of
" Pop " with much dignity arise, and smite
this democrat " hip and thigh," by inditing
an answer in the next week's *Chronicle*,
averring that the insinuations were those of
some envious boy who could not get elected
to "Pop," concluding with the remark that
" what is, must be best "—a conservative
expression of opinion that in those days
went to the heart of Etonians.

Ere another quarter has boomed forth
from the old clock in college yard, we are
conscious of a dull tramping sound, like the
regular advance of a battalion of infantry;
but wending our way towards Barnes Pool
(the former boundary of Eton), we become
aware of a long line of boys, sitting thick
as a string of bees on a low wall, against
which they are beating time with their
heels.

An elderly man standing by, being a
stranger to old Eton customs, fails to imagine why the boys should congregate in the
narrowest part of the street, with no greater
attraction, apparently, than a view of the
booksellers' windows, and the unlovely dark
wire-blind which conceals the edibles in
Joseph Brown's " sock " shop.

He does not long remain in ignorance, for
presently cheers ring out from hundreds of
lusty young throats, and a crowd of boys,
hat in hand, come running down the street,
shouting loudly the while.

Four stalwart youths, bareheaded, sur-

round an individual—two seize each a
white-trousered leg, two more support his
head and shoulders, bearing him swiftly
along, heated and panting, the very picture
of discomfort. " Ah ! " doubtless thinks the
stranger, " some malefactor caught red-
handed by the boys, and they are carrying
him to the police-station." But no ; see,
the bearers, after traversing a hundred yards
with their burthen, turn, retrace their steps
at the same rapid pace to the starting-point
at Barnes Pool, the crowd on the wall
shrieking out shrill approval.

The puzzled stranger is fain to turn to
a youth with an irreproachably starched
white tie and glossy hat for explanation of
this strange scene ; but the youth addressed
is lost in reverie, perhaps wondering if he
will ever be carried in like fashion " for
valour," and does not reply. A bright,
cherry-cheeked boy beside him, however,
who has been alternately cheering and
solacing himself with such refreshment as
some very doubtful-looking butter-scotch

could afford, is eager, being a new-comer
that term, not to appear a tyro, and supplies
the desired information as if he were indeed
"Past master" of Eton customs.

"You see," quoth he, " we licked Winchester like anything; and now they are
hoisting the two captains, and the fellows
who made the biggest scores in the match.
Look out! Here they come again!" and
little Rawson, in his excitement, lets fall
his treasured piece of butter-scotch.

Several boys in dark-blue caps are in turn
borne up and down the street, and the
Etonians, in all courtesy, cheer their late
opponents. Then, the Eton captain is
carried along, and the shouting may perhaps be a shade more prolonged. But now
arises a louder cheer than any as yet heard,
and in answer to the eager query from those
on the wall, the name of "Wynyard!" is
yelled out, and it is evident that here is the
favourite hero of the day.

The boys with one accord scramble up,
and stand on the wall. Cheer after cheer

rings out from hundreds of willing young throats, and when Wynyard and his bearers reach the turning-point, in their enthusiasm the boys thump on their hats, leap down from the wall, and rush frantically down the street after their favourite. Even the stranger is seized with the general enthusiasm, and waves his hat, cheering with the rest. Long after Wynyard. has reached Barnes Pool, the hurrahs are prolonged, and the " one cheer more " extends to many before the excitement at all subsides.

Ah, Dick Wynyard! you are destined to be petted and made much of when you grow to man's estate, but never in your life will you receive the sincere flattery you are hearing from those honest young voices to-day.

Several others of the Eton eleven receive their meed of praise in the shape of hoisting, but the cheers, albeit hearty, are fainter than before; and the stranger, an elderly man, with long grizzled beard and sun-tanned skin, turns again to little Rawson, and inquires who was the boy hoisted after the Eton captain, not having caught his name.

"Ah!" said Rawson, "he is such a jolly fellow; he boards at my dame's house. Not very good at 'sap,' you know; but he will do verses for any lower boy; and though they are always wrong, yet we know he tries to help us. He would be captain of the eleven, but he is so low down in the school; then he is the best fives player, and he played for Eton in the racket matches at Prince's last year; and he is 'flying man' in the 'field,' and can kick a football farther than any one in the school. Then, Mr. Barre says that, if he did not play cricket, he rows well enough to be in the eight to go to Henley."

"An Admirable Crichton, indeed," said the stranger, "in all save the classics. What is his name, by-the-by?"

"Why, Wynyard, of course," replied Rawson, as if astonished that any one should ask such a question.

"Wynyard?" repeated the stranger with some show of interest. "Is his name Richard?" and on receiving an answer in the affirmative, said, half to himself, "Why, this must be the nephew I came down to see."

Two or three boys had overheard the conversation, and it soon spread that Wynyard's uncle was there; and he, though quite unconscious of the fact, immediately became an object of interest, not to say admiration, to the youthful crowd as he sauntered slowly off towards Windsor.

The hoisting is over, and now the crowd about Barnes Pool is thinning, as the boys walk away to their respective houses to be in time for "lock up."

Two of the Eton eleven stroll slowly away together. The taller of the two is a slim, dark youth, of somewhat sallow complexion—a complete contrast to his companion, who, with sunny chestnut hair, kindly blue eyes, broad-chested and sunburnt, is the beau-ideal of a young Englishman. The dark lad is Reginald Burton, the

Eton captain; the other his cousin, Dick Wynyard.

Both are silent as they walk along, each occupied with his own thoughts, which are widely different. Burton, always jealous of his handsome, stalwart cousin, is this evening especially sore, for he had easily detected that the cheers for Wynyard were heartier than those given in his own honour. Honest Dick, on the contrary, well pleased with himself, and envying no one, was thinking how he had enjoyed his day's cricket, and devoutly hoping he may not be put on to construe Xenophon on the Monday.

Burton is the first to break the silence, and exclaims, somewhat peevishly, " Well, I must say, Dick, you did have tremendous luck in getting such a score to-day. You ought to have been caught at least three times, and that wicket-keeper missed stumping you before you had made twenty runs."

Dick turns with a pleasant smile, and either not or affecting not to notice the ill-natured tone in which his cousin speaks, says cheerily, " Well, I did have some luck, to be sure, old fellow; but, then, the catches were very hard ones, you know. But, by Jove! if you hadn't gone on to bowl, we should never have won the match. Those break-backs of yours regularly beat them ; " and he lays his hand kindly on the other's shoulder as he speaks.

Burton thaws visibly, mollified by the praise of his bowling, of which he is very vain. Indeed, Mr. Satchell had once said of him, sarcastically, " If Burton could only really bowl as well as he thinks he can, no eleven could be found to play against him."

But there is no time for more words, for the lock-up bell sounds from several houses, and Burton will have to hurry to reach his tutor's in time ; so, with a hasty " Good night!—see you to-morrow," he runs off.

Wynyard has only a few yards to go before reaching his dame's house. As he goes under the old archway several boys give a shrill hurrah; but he holds up his

hand warningly, and says, " Don't make a
row, you fellows, for my dame's not well,
I know, and you may disturb her."

It was this kindly feeling, ever shown to
all, almost as much as his skill at games,
which made him the idol of his companions.

Even his grim tutor, when inclined to
wax wrath at some incorrigible fit of lazi-
ness, could not resist the rare charm of
Wynyard's smile.

CHAPTER II.

AT MISS GELLATLY'S.

"Ah, happy years! once more
Who would not be a boy?"

BYRON.

WYNYARD runs lightly up the stairs and into his own room.

It is a small chamber. A bedstead, which folds up into a cupboard by day, stands in one corner, flanked by a bureau, the lower half of which forms a chest of drawers; and these, with three. chairs, constitute his necessary furniture.

A gaudy painting of a fair equestrian, attired in light-green habit, who is "flying" an impossible "double" on a flame-coloured horse, hangs near the window, and the rest of the pictures indicate the sporting tastes of the owner.

The place of honour over the mantelpiece is occupied by a large coloured photograph, which is easily recognized as Wynyard's mother, from the strong likeness it bears to her son. And yet there is a perceptible difference in the character of the two faces. Both have the same truthful, honest blue eyes, and hair of golden brown—in one, now thickly flecked with white; but in the mother the nose is more aquiline, the chin finer and stronger, and the thin lips pressed firmly together give an almost stern expression to the face altogether absent from the son's.

Lady Nora had been a beauty before her marriage, and now, in the autumn of her life, the shades are but mellowed and subdued. The roses may not bloom so brightly in her cheeks, nor the eyes sparkle with the fire of twenty years ago; but there is a nameless grace in every movement, and albeit unconsciously a little stately in manner from the retired life she leads now, there is a charm in her somewhat sad smile that none can resist. The poor on the estates simply worship her. Many a sick bed has been soothed by her kindly presence and low, soft voice; and the cotters are never weary of telling tales of her bountiful goodness to all who are ill or in trouble.

Lady Nora was the only daughter of the Earl of Kilrood, an improvident Irish peer, whose rent-roll was unfortunately not so long as his pedigree. Five and twenty years before our story opens, Lord Kilrood, broken in health and spirit, sick of a world in which he could no longer play a part, because of insufficient means, had betaken himself to a half-ruined castle on the west coast of Ireland—the only property he could not alienate—and there had lived out the rest of a disappointed life.

Few remembered him as the smart young guardsman of nearly forty years before; and when, two years later, the news of his death

was read out at the Pabulum (the club
he had most affected in his lifetime), it was
only as of one more broken-down old man
" gone over to the majority " that they
thought of him.

Henry Chutney indeed, a cynical member
of a Government office, whose savage sar-
casms were dreaded by his junior clerks, on
coming into the card-room of the Pabulum
for his usual afternoon whist, was told of
the death of his whilom acquaintance, and
observed, " So old Kilrood is gone, is he ?
Well, I must say that's about the best thing
he ever did in his life ! Now then, who's
for a rubber ? Don't all speak at once ! "

And thus was his requiem sung at the
Pabulum. Ere a week had passed he was
completely forgotten, as if he had never
lived, as have been many better and worse
men before him.

His daughter, after the first shock, did
not grieve very deeply. Indeed, no one
could have accused Lord Kilrood of being a
domestic character, and after the death of

his wife (a beautiful Frenchwoman to whom he had been passionately attached), father and daughter met but seldom. The girl had been sent to live with an aunt after her mother's death, and there she had remained until her marriage. The mother's fortune, some £1200 a year, had been settled on her child, so happily she had not been dependent on her improvident old sire.

Aunt and niece did not get on very well together. The former, a worldly woman who had married for money herself, strove to impress upon her niece the desirability of doing likewise; but Nora, rather romantic at that time, was determined not to bestow her hand without her heart, and nearly drove poor Lady Bullion frantic by the cool way in which she dismissed two very eligible *partis* in her first season. The men admired her intensely, and her passage through a ball-room resembled a royal progress, so eager were all to obtain a dance before every valse was given away.

Her cousin, Captain Wynyard (" Blarney

Dick," as he was dubbed in the —th Lancers), was her constant companion, and when, at the end of Nora's second season in London, their engagement was announced, no one was astonished except Lady Bullion.

That worthy woman shed a few tears over her niece's perversity, as she termed it, but ended by being reconciled to the match after an hour's conversation with Captain Wynyard, during which that fascinating *sabreur* praised her house, her taste in dress, by delicate implication herself, and even adroitly hinted that *she* had been the promoter of the match.

What more could the vanity of a chaperone require? Captain Dick took his hat and his leave, feeling that the goodwill of Lady Bullion was assured.

The cousins were married in August. Before Christmas, which they passed at his father's place in Oxfordshire, Captain Wynyard began to think that he was "not cut out for a Benedict," as he himself expressed it, and soon the handsome but erratic lancer found that the arduous duties of his profession compelled him to be much away from home.

As Dick was somewhat of a scamp, need we say that his wife had loved him very dearly; and when, in the following year, war was declared against Russia, and her husband's regiment was ordered out to the Crimea, Nora was nearly frantic with grief. Her worst fears were realized. She never saw him again. Captain Wynyard was shot through the heart by a Russian bullet, riding at the head of his troop in that fatal charge at Balaclava.

They broke the news of his death as tenderly as possible to his widow. She did not weep, as at their parting, but seemed stunned by the blow, and at first they feared for her brain, so unnatural did this deathly calm appear. For three days and nights her life trembled in the balance, and then her son was born. From that hour Nora rallied and grew stronger, as if that tiny life had given her something to live for, and in less than a fortnight she was pronounced convalescent — the only change outwardly being, that in her hair were "silver threads amongst the gold."

Old Squire Wynyard, much shaken and aged since his son's death, died the following year, and thenceforward Lady Nora lived almost entirely at High Wynyard. Suitors were not wanting after her year of mourning had expired; but she told them, one and all, that she should never marry again. And she kept her word — devoting her life to the poor, and her boy's education. It was a bitter pang to her when Dick grew old enough to be sent to Eton, but she felt it was for his good, and nerved herself to part with him for the first time since his birth. She cried when the time came for saying good-bye, filled his purse (knitted by her own hands) much fuller than it should have been, and with the hamper that was sent to him with edibles for his breakfast the following week, was the portrait which has attracted our notice over Dick's mantelpiece.

CHAPTER III.

DICK RECEIVES A LETTER.

"O my prophetic soul ! mine uncle !"

SHAKESPEARE.

THE boys at Miss Gellatly's are busily engaged over their supper, at which honest Dick takes as vigorous a part as in the match against Winchester. If, indeed, that lady is suffering, as Wynyard had announced on his entry, the ceaseless chatter kept up anent the cricket match can scarcely be soothing to her nerves.

But all things have an end (even suppers, as that worthy dame is pleased to find), and presently the room is cleared for evening prayers, which the head boy of the house reads out—I fear to rather an inattentive

congregation—and then the boys troop upstairs to bed as the lights are turned off
below.

Dick, on entering his room, becomes
aware of a letter lying on the table, which
we will take the liberty of reading over his
shoulder.

It ran as follows :—

" White Hart Hotel, Windsor.

" MY DEAR NEPHEW,

" I have made your acquaintance
epistolarily, through your letters to your
mother, which she was good enough to
forward to me sometimes out in America.
I paid her a visit at High Wynyard on my
arrival in England about a fortnight ago,
and, learning that you were at Eton, determined to run down and make the
personal acquaintance of my nephew and
ward.

" I was too late to see your innings in
the Winchester match, but I did witness
your triumph later on in the hoisting,

when I trust that you were not so uncomfortable as your position looked to me
to be. The old saw says there are 'no
roses without thorns;' therefore, no doubt,
you endured the discomfort willingly, for
the sake of the glory it entailed.

"My object in writing is to ask you to
breakfast with me . here, at nine o'clock
to-morrow morning, and, as I do not
know his address, would you ask my other
nephew, Reggie Burton, to accompany you
to see

     "Your affectionate uncle,

       "THOMAS LOUGHTON WYNYARD.

"Saturday night."

"And so here's Uncle Tom come back
from America at last," thought Wynyard;
"and what a rummy letter he writes, by Gad!
What's all this about roses and thorns, and
whatever have they got to do with hoisting,
I should like to know? Burton's a clever
chap, perhaps he'll make it out. Anyhow,
I must write to tell him about the break-

fast—so here goes." And Dick sat down with a sigh, and indited a note as follows :—

" Miss Gellatly's, Eton College.

" DEAR BURTON,

"Uncle Tom has turned up at last from America, and is stopping at the White Hart. He wants us both to breakfast with him to-morrow morning, so will you call for me at eight, sharp, and we'll go together.

"Yours always,

"R. M. WYNYARD."

Then he goes out into the passage and roars, " Lower boy !" Several come, obedient to his call, and selecting one, Wynyard says, " Here, Green minor, just take this note to Burton at Towler's to-morrow morning early, will you ? "

" All right," said the fag, taking the note, glad of an opportunity to serve the great man, and vanished to the upper regions.

Dick goes back into his own room, and after first taking up a book and putting it

down, whistling low the while, subsides into
a hard-backed Windsor chair, places his legs
on the table, and in that elegant attitude
proceeds to think about that Uncle Tom
whom he has, as yet, not seen. Of course
he inclines to the warlike, and pictures his
relative with sweeping moustache and com-
manding figure. Then he gets up and looks
in the glass anxiously at his own hirsute
appendages, which are just budding; and
apparently the result is satisfactory, for
there is a smile on his comely face when
he turns again and proceeds to undress, pre-
paratory to retiring to his well-earned re-
pose. We will leave him to unrobe, and
give the reader a slight sketch of that
Uncle Tom to whom he will be presented
on the morrow.

Tom Wynyard's father had occupied himself during his lifetime in the unsuccessful
attempt to establish a claim to the baronetcy which had lain dormant in his family
for three generations; but like Sir Pitt
Crawley, of whom Lord Steyne said that

"he always ratted at the wrong moment,"
so Mr. Wynyard never obtained the baronetcy he coveted, because neither Government were ever sure of his support in his
county.   He was too much engrossed in
this and other schemes to pay much attention to giving his sons a profession, and
when the old man died, Tom Wynyard
found himself without a home, and possessed of the very moderate younger son's
portion of six thousand pounds.

However, he was endowed with admirable health, indomitable pluck, and a de-
termination, as his way in the world had
not been made for him, to show that
he could be the architect of his own
fortunes.

Three months after his father's death,
Tom Wynyard was landed at New York,
armed with a letter of introduction to a
mercantile house at Chicago, where he in
due course arrived, and was taken into the
firm, at first with no salary. But his shrewd
American employer soon saw his capa-

bilities. He "liked the youngster," he averred; "his head was screwed on the right way, and there was no darned conceit about him." So the lad was advanced from time to time, until he was sent to manage a branch house in San Francisco. By this time Wynyard was a partner in the firm, and, as he was allowed to speculate on his own account, took some shares in mines, purchased a tract of land through which the railway was brought shortly afterwards, and in eighteen years from the time he landed his various securities represented several million dollars.

During all this time Tom Wynyard had corresponded little with his relations. Liking the life in San Francisco, and keenly devoted to sport, he remained there; and instead of going to Europe for relaxation, travelled in the South American republics.

But after a time a yearning came over him to see the old country again; and without abandoning his interests in America,

Mr. Wynyard sailed for England (professedly on a year's visit), and had landed in Liverpool about a fortnight before we saw him this evening in Eton.

CHAPTER IV.

UNCLE TOM.

"In morals blameless as in manners meek,
He knew no thought that he might blush to speak."
COWPER.

BURTON arrived at Miss Gellatly's the following morning, and made his way up to Dick's room.

To his annoyance he finds that indolent youth fast asleep, and, judging from the smile on his parted lips, fighting the battle of yesterday over again in his dreams.

His cousin, however, ruthlessly dispels these illusions by unceremoniously seizing him by the shoulders and shaking him until he opens his eyes.

Wynyard awakes with a start; and recognizing Burton, says, somewhat sleepily—

"Hullo! old chap—you here already? Why, what time is it?"

"A quarter past eight, and you told me to be here at eight, sharp," replied Burton, in an aggrieved tone; "we shall be awfully late for Uncle Tom's breakfast!"

"Not a bit of it," returned Dick cheerily, in no way abashed by the implied reproof. "Just take a book, will you, and I'll be ready in a brace of shakes;" and as he speaks Dick jumps into his cold tub, from which he presently emerges glowing and breathless, and proceeds rapidly to array himself in Sunday apparel.

Burton meanwhile has been glancing round the room, and bestowing a contemptuous sniff of disapproval on the lady in green and her flame-coloured horse, turns to the mantelpiece, whereon are displayed sundry silver and pewter cups, of which some had been won by Wynyard at fives and others for rowing and athletics. Eyeing these trophies askance, Burton said, "Why don't you keep the money, instead of always getting cups, when you win?"

"Well, you see," replied Dick, with a pin in his mouth and mind intent on the tying of a spotless white cravat, "I don't want the tin, and they will make a jolly addition to the old racing cups at home. Besides," he added, with a merry twinkle in his eye, "I am not so steady as you, old boy, and the tin soon melts with me."

Burton snorts aggressively. Indeed, it was another grievance with this young gentleman that his handsome cousin should have been born with a golden spoon in his mouth, whereas his own, figuratively, was of baser metal.

Burton was the son of a hard-working lawyer—much thought of, indeed, in his profession, but with a large family to provide for, and Reginald, though the eldest, will, as he knows, have to work for his living.

Dick, of course, had inherited the High Wynyard property, on the death of his grandfather.   His mother had carefully nursed the estates during his long minority, so that an ample fortune will be at Dick's command when he comes of age.

That cheerful individual gives a final smooth to his curly locks, puts on his coat, and announces that he is ready for a start, and the two cousins go out together.

There is no time for much conversation as they walk hurriedly along the High Street and over Windsor Bridge, but Burton remarks that he has heard Uncle Tom has made a large fortune in America, and wonders what he will do with it.

Dick replies that he " don't care one button whether Uncle Tom is rich or not," but opines " that he is a jolly good fellow to come down to see his nephews."

By this time they are passing the Hundred Steps and venerable Curfew Tower ; a few yards further brings them to the doors of the White Hart, and Burton as spokesman asks the waiter for Mr. Wynyard.

" Yessir," replies that trim functionary.

"This way, sir, please; breakfast quite ready, sir," and ushers the pair (Dick speculating as to whether this knight of the napkin could be brought to say "No, sir") into a sitting-room on the first floor.

Here is laid out a well-spread breakfast table. Presently the door of an adjoining bedroom opens, and the stranger of yesterday evening walks in.

He looks keenly at the two lads, and then, extending his hand to Wynyard, says cordially—

"No need to ask which is which, for I can tell that you are Dick from the likeness to your dear mother." Then, turning to Burton, he congratulates him on the Eton victory of yesterday, and expresses gratification that a nephew of his should be captain of the eleven.

The three then sit down to breakfast, and naturally the conversation is of the cricket match. Uncle Tom, with a look of quiet enjoyment on his weather-beaten face, listens attentively to the remarks of the two lads, only occasionally cutting in with some shrewd observation or joke on their delicate appetites.

At last, even Dick protests that he can eat no more strawberries and cream, and Uncle Tom says—

" Now, boys, I have got leave from the head master for you both. How can we pass the day? Shall we row up to Monkey Island and lunch there?"

" We always go to chapel on Sundays," begins Burton, rather priggishly; but Uncle Tom cuts him short somewhat sharply, and decides that they shall go to chapel in the morning and row up to Monkey in the afternoon.

Mr. Wynyard lights a huge cheroot, and the three walk together down Eton as the bells begin to peal. They enter the grand old chapel; the boys go to their respective seats, Uncle Tom being conducted to a stall next one of the masters of the college, by a verger with silver rod.

After the service, uncle and nephews wend

their way to Windsor Bridge, take a boat
from Goodman's Raft, which the boys row,
Uncle Tom steering, with a calm disregard
for the sides of the river which more than
once brings them into jeopardy. However,
they escape actual collision, and Uncle
Tom, leaning back amongst the cushions,
thoroughly enjoys the scenery, and is keenly
interested when the boys point out the
different places of note as they glide
swiftly by. "Upper Hope" and "Athens,"
the school bathing-places, are soon passed,
and then they go through the lock by
Boveney Weir.

After this "Surly Hall" is reached, and
Dick tells his uncle of the glories of the 4th
of June, when the boats row up in pro-
cession to dine, the cricket eleven faring
sumptuously in a tent hard by. The boys
speak regretfully of the past glories of the
4th, and anticipate the coming delights of
"Election Saturday."

And so they row swiftly on, until at last
they step out and fasten up their boat at

Monkey Island, where they lunch and gather roses, then float quietly down the stream in the cool twilight; Uncle Tom recounting tales to the delighted lads of his American adventures, smoking innumerable cheroots the while.

When they reach Goodman's Raft once more, the boys take leave of their uncle (who returns to London the following day), and I am not sure that a tear did not glisten in poor old Uncle Tom's eye; and his voice is a little husky as he wishes them good-bye, pressing at the same time a bank-note into the hand of each.

As they walk back to Eton, Dick emphatically states his opinion that " Uncle Tom is a regular brick; " and even Burton, with that crisp note rustling pleasantly in his waistcoat pocket, admits that Mr. Wynyard " seems rather good-natured."

Both boys are tired when they reach their respective houses. Burton, indeed, conscientiously prepares his task for the morrow before retiring to rest; but heed-

less Dick goes straight to bed, calmly
ignoring the fact that he has forty lines of
Virgil to say by heart the following morning, not one word of which has he even
glanced at.

CHAPTER V.

AT LORD'S.

" Tho' from truth I haply err,
The scene presents its character."
                                    COMBE.

TIME seems to have only crept along since
the Winchester match—so think Wynyard
and Burton—and the latter has expressed
a wish that he could seize the ruthless old
scythe-bearer (who marches all too quickly
for most of us) by the forelock and force
him to hasten his footsteps.

But at last the longed-for day of the
Harrow match dawns, and a brilliant sun
shines on eleven happy young faces as they
drive off in Charley Wise's break, *en route*
for London.

The metropolis reached, Mr. Satchell and

Mr. George, with an anxious look on their countenances (for are we not on the eve of a battle?), marshal their forces, and take them off to Lord's cricket-ground, where the Harrow eleven are already arrived.

Uncle Tom, seated in a hansom-cab about one o'clock, on his way to keep an appointment in Porchester Terrace, thinks, as he is driven up Baker Street, that he has never before seen so many vehicles in that gloomy thoroughfare, and notices, with some curiosity, that all seem to be coming from the same direction; moreover, that most are empty. However, he is engrossed with his own thoughts, and it is only on arriving opposite St. John's Wood Station that he becomes aware that, for some unknown reason, his cab is proceeding at only a foot's pace behind a long line of others.

Leaning forward to indignantly remonstrate, Mr. Wynyard inquired of a policeman standing in the road the reason of the block.

That long-suffering official, hot and dusty,

thirsting for his usual mid-day glass of "bitter," sulkily replied, " Why, the Eton an' 'Arrer match, in course—and a precious nice job it is, too," he added, sarcastically.

" Good heavens ! " excitedly exclaims Uncle Tom. " The Eton and Harrow match to-day ! Why, I've two nephews playing ! " And casting all thoughts of business to the winds, he shouts through the trap-door to his amused Jehu, " Stop at Lord's, cabby." Then, taking out a card, he hastily scrawls an excuse on the back, and gives it to the cabman on arriving at the gate of Lord's ground, with directions to leave it at Porchester Terrace.

Let us follow him in as he pays his half-crown at the turnstile, and buys a card of the match from an urchin in the scarlet cap of the Marylebone Club.

A glance at the field and the telegraph-board shows us that Harrow have the first innings, and that five wickets have fallen for a hundred and twenty-seven runs. It is a curious sight. Ropes run round the

space allotted to the cricketers, and behind
these sit boys and men, keenly watching
every incident in the game; the boys ap-
plauding every run, or well-pitched ball that
nearly finds its way to the batsman's wicket.
Loud are the cheers at a brilliant piece of
fielding, and unmerciful the banter if a
swift ball pass through longstop's legs. Impervious indeed to sarcasm should be that
Eton cover-point, for a catch comes straight
and hard which that unlucky youth fails to
hold; and what reproof could be more
galling than the ironical "Ah, butter-
fingers!" from a shrill Harrow voice which
greets this mishap?

But the sky is overcast, and a few drops
of rain fall. Quickly all round the ring
umbrellas are hoisted, looking like rows of
gigantic mushrooms. Only a few heat-
spots, however, and they are soon furled
again.

Let us stroll round outside the ropes and
look at the carriages and their occupants.

Here are fair women in gauzy dresses of

every imaginable colour—though light blue
seems to predominate—and brave men who
if not exactly clad in "purple and fine
linen," perhaps it is only because broad-
cloth of that gorgeous hue is not in vogue.
Near the pavilion, behind the spectators,
is a line of coaches drawn up closely together.   The roof of this blue one, picked
out with red, supports some of the House-
hold Brigade, each with an exotic in his
button-hole, and brilliantly varnished boots.
On the box-seat of that yellow coach, cigar
in mouth, sits a jaunty baronet, with half
a yard of pocket-handkerchief hanging from
the pocket of his brown coat with the
Four-in-hand Club buttons.   Here, walking
arm-in-arm, are the well-known figures of
a handsome but choleric north-country
M.F.H., and the popular member for Eborton.   Close behind appears the smiling,
good-natured face and portly form of Mr.
Shenley, who represents the thriving town
of Ribbonton in the Senate.   One of the
best whips of the day is Mr. Shenley, and

accounted the smartest-dressed member of the " House."

At the corner we are nearly run over by a victoria, drawn by a white horse, in which are seated a popular actor and his charming wife; and continuing our way round by the racket-court, we come across many a well-known face seen nearly every day, as well as many met with only on this occasion every year. Indeed, as we pass by one of the drags of the Coaching Club, we overhear a youth —irreproachably dressed in a light-coloured suit, with white hat to match—gravely assuring a fair damsel, who had never once looked at the cricket, that " all London was on the ground! "

On the roofs of coaches, on tables ex-temporized behind the carriages, elaborate luncheons are being laid out by liveried servants. Lobsters and chickens, creamy mayonnaise, huge raised pies and fruit, sur-round us; and the necks of champagne bottles peep temptingly out from ice-pails on all sides.

A shrill scream from a little Etonian of
"Bowled!—well bowled indeed!" just at
our ear, makes us start violently round, in
time to see the cricketers retiring to the
pavilion; and a glance at the telegraph-
board shows that the last Harrow wicket is
down, with the total at a hundred and sixty-
three.

The crowd, tired of sitting, spread out
over the ground when the cricketers have
retired; and presently the genial secretary
of the M.C.C. announces that, as it is nearly
two o'clock, the boys will lunch before
beginning the Eton innings.

The popping of champagne corks is now
heard on all sides, and soon most are busily
engaged in discussing luncheon, and a little
mild wagering, principally in gloves, takes
place between the partisans of the two
schools.

"Oh, I do so hope Eton will win!" says
a pretty fair-haired girl to a somewhat
stolid-looking dragoon, who is helping her
to champagne.

"Why?" inquires rather gruffly that son of Mars, who sports the dark-blue colours of the other school. "Your two brothers were both at Harrow, so you oughtn't to back Eton."

"But I don't care the least for that," returns the damsel, affecting a little *moue* of displeasure; "and I am going to wear a light-blue dress to-morrow, because the shade is so much more becoming than that horrid dark blue; so I do hope Eton will win."

They are sitting at the back of a coach, and the soldier leans over and whispers into the little pink ear. What he says no one overhears; but apparently he makes his peace, for she looks up once—only once—into his face, and a little hand steals for a moment into his broad palm under cover of her shawl.

Happy dragoon! take care of your tender little plant; you need not fear any rival henceforth in her affections.

But now the bell is ringing once more to

clear the ground, and in a few minutes the cricketers come out again from the pavilion.

Alas! for Eton hopes; the very first ball—a regular trimmer—just takes off the bails, and poor Anton has to walk disconsolately back to the pavilion with a huge " duck's-egg " to his credit, instead of the dozen runs at least he had hoped would figure opposite his name in the scoring-sheet.

Who is this who strides out from the pavilion padded and gloved, swinging his bat carelessly as he walks along? Why, Wynyard, to be sure. Ah, now we shall see some play.

But Dick blocks the first two balls very carefully, and then a loose one is bowled, which he cuts hard to the boundary for three, evoking a hearty cheer from the partisans of Eton.

At this point, to our annoyance, a friend meets us with a telegram, which forces us to leave the ground immediately, and we see no more of the game that day. Eagerly we scan the evening papers at the club, and see that Wynyard carried out his bat for seventy-four runs; Burton, the captain, played steadily for a neat nineteen, but the Eton total only amounted to a hundred and fifty-six, leaving Harrow seven runs to the good on the first innings.

CHAPTER VI.

THE SECOND DAY OF THE MATCH.

" Conquer we shall, but we must first contend ;
'Tis not the fight that crowns us, but the end."
HERRICK, *Hesperides.*

THE next morning, big with the fate of
Eton and Harrow, dawns brilliantly, and at
an early hour thousands are making their
way up to the cricket-ground.

Uncle Tom, feeling at least ten years
younger, is at Lord's, excited as any school-
boy, long before the commencement of hos-
tilities. To atone for his forgetfulness of
yesterday, he has a huge light-blue rosette
in his button-hole, and a bow of the same
coloured ribbon is tied in a conspicuous
place on his umbrella.

At eleven o'clock the bell rings, and the two Harrow champions, in dark blue and white-striped caps, come first down the pavilion steps, quickly followed by the Eton eleven and the umpires. In a few minutes play begins in earnest.

We watch a few overs bowled, and then, feeling that cricket does not interest us so keenly as twenty years ago, stroll round the ground and go into the tennis-court, where we watch that interesting game for an hour, and then pass on to the gallery of the racket-court.

By the time that we return, the telegraph-board shows that six Harrow wickets have fallen for only eighty-seven runs, and before luncheon time the whole eleven are out for a hundred and thirty-two—leaving Eton a hundred and thirty-nine runs to get to win.

The Rev. Mr. Satchell, of Eton, and Mr. Brimstone (the Harrow coach) are standing together on the pavilion steps, and the former feels that now is victory almost within his grasp.

"Wait a bit," says Mr. Brimstone quietly, "until you see what our fielding is like when it comes to a tussle."

As he speaks the cricketers come out again. Anton and Munby are again in first, and both lads play steadily and well until the score mounts gradually up to twenty-eight, with no wicket down. Then Munby incautiously steps out to a "half volley," misses it, and in an instant the bails are off.

" How's that ? " asks the wicket-keeper.

" Out ! " returns the umpire ; and Munby retires with eighteen to his credit, Burton filling the vacant wicket.

At luncheon time only three wickets are down for seventy-eight runs, and Mr. Satchell is jubilant. We dare not suggest that that reverend gentleman has made a bet with Mr. Brimstone on the issue of the match, but there is a satisfied look on his face which we have noticed at race meetings on the countenances of "backers" when the commission is well "on." Who can affirm that the worthy man has not

risked the modest stake of a new " beaver "
on the result ?

Luncheon over, like giants refreshed,
Burton and his partner resume the offen-
sive, the former playing steadily and well ;
but a catch at square leg disposes of his
vis-à-vis. And now the two cousins face
one another.

Burton plays the rest of the over without
scoring, and then Wynyard prepares to
defend his wicket against the insidious
slows of the Harrow captain.

Dick blocks the first two balls with ex-
emplary caution, and then lets out at a
loose one to leg.

" Run ! " cries Burton, and then—was it
accident or design ?—he stops and shouts,
" No, no, go back ; no run there ! "

Dick, who has reached the middle of the
pitch, turns, slips, and tries to get back to
his wicket in time ; but the ball has been
well fielded, and sharply returned by short
leg : before he can reach the fatal crease, a
Harrow shout announces that his wicket is

down, and the crack bat of Eton is "run
out" without scoring.

Dick, as he walks back to the pavilion,
feels a hard lump rising in his throat; he
bravely tries to choke it down, but he hardly
distinguishes the sea of commiserating faces,
for, do what he will to keep them back, a
salt tear will rise in either eye. He strides
into the pavilion, and feels very miserable
as he slowly unbuckles his pads and puts
away the shoes that have played him false.
But the instincts of breed are strong within
him, and there is not a trace of regret on
his comely face as he laughingly accepts
the condolences of his friends, and sits down
on the bench to watch the game.

Meanwhile affairs are looking very black
for Eton. Terry has succumbed to the
insidious slows, and now six of the best
wickets are down for only ninety-six runs.

"We shall never do it now," says poor
Mr. Satchell.

The Harrow fielding at this juncture is
superb. Run after run is saved, and "long

leg" on either side cover so much ground that they seem to be everywhere the ball is hit to.

Burton is playing with remarkable patience, but these tactics do not suit Staunton, the noted "slogger" of the eleven. A half volley comes; Staunton steps out, open his shoulders, and drives the ball grandly right over the very flagstaff on the roof of the pavilion—a magnificent hit, which brings a hundred upon the board, accompanied by a howl of delight from Eton boys.

But alas! for the vanity of human nature. Staunton, elated by his success, strives to eclipse his grand drive. He steps out, but the bowler craftily sends down a short-pitched ball, which Staunton sends twisting up into the air, only to find a safe resting-place in cover-point's hands.

"All over, except shouting," chuckles Mr. Brimstone, and compliments Staunton on his splendid hit.

"Ah!" returned that unabashed youth,

"I didn't half catch hold of it, though!"
which provokes a roar of laughter from the
pavilion benches.

The new-comer begins well with a couple
of twos, and Burton in the next over gets a
late cut for three. This, with another brace
of twos and a bye, brings the score up to a
hundred and sixteen, and Eton hopes are
once more raised—only to be dashed, however, for Burton hits the next ball to leg
hard and high in the direction of the
racket-court (will it go over the heads of
the spectators ?), and this fine hits evokes a
cheer from Eton, quickly drowned by a
deafening counter-cheer from Harrow, as
" long leg " runs about fifteen yards, leaps
up, and catches the ball in one hand.

Burton retires, having played a patient
and useful innings of thirty-seven. And
now, indeed, the captain gone, does there
seem no hope for Eton.

However, Field, the new-comer, plays
with a confidence and ease that fairly
astonishes his friends. He gives each

bowler a 'taste of his quality by a couple of drives for two in one over; and in the next a cut for the same amount, a leg hit for three, and a few singles, bring very shortly a hundred and thirty up on the telegraph board.   Field, however, burning to distinguish himself, hits wildly at a short-pitched ball, which drops easily into long-slip's hands.

The last two boys are in, and still eight runs have to be obtained before they equal the Harrow score.   It seems impossible.

The excitement is intense.   Every ball evokes a shout from Harrow partisans of "Well bowled!" answered by an Eton cheer of "Well played!" as the batsman blocks a dangerous "shooter."

Etches, the last man in (acting, possibly, on the directions of Mr. Satchell), steals a bye—and another.   The longstop loses his temper, throws wildly at the wicket, and amidst shouts of "Run it out!" from Eton, the batsmen run two more for the over-throw.

A change of bowling is tried as a last resource, but the batsmen are not to be tempted to "slog," and cautiously block every straight ball, playing with admirable nerve and patience.

And now the score has crept gradually up until Eton are but one run behind their antagonists. The boys looking on hardly breathe, until Etches make a forward drive for two, and, amidst a scene of the wildest excitement, wins the match for Eton.

The Eton boys leap over the ropes, make a rush at Etches, and carry him triumphantly to the pavilion. There they form a crowd, cheering and shouting for their favourites to come out.

It is an hour before the excitement at all subsides, and there is a considerable difficulty in getting away from the ground; consequently we find time to notice that the light-blue colours seem to be almost universally sported, and we do not remember that such was the case in the morning.

A straw shows which way the wind blows, it is said.   May we not say that the colours sported after the Eton and Harrow match show which way the victory has gone ?

CHAPTER VII.

VALE ETONA.

"Farewell, O Cuckoo Weir, whose banks I used to court!
Farewell, O playing-fields, wherein I loved to sport!
To dive from high Acropolis and cleave the pliant wave."

THE curtain is nearly down—the last act
almost played out on the Eton stage.
Burton and Wynyard both leave the old
college for good at the end of the term.

Wynyard, as the highest individual scorer
against Harrow—and a good customer—has
been presented with a bat by Mr. Ferry,
the enterprising vendor of footballs and
china, perfumery and pictures (what, indeed,
does that great and good man not sell?),
with the inscription, "From Frizzles," at
the back, on a silver plate. And for the

hoisting after the match, and the subsequent festivities of Election Saturday, are they not writ in the annals of Eton chronicles far better than we can portray them?

Dick has been presented also with over a hundred "Leaving Books"—gaudy of binding, indeed, but utterly guiltless of interest inside—as mementos of his schoolfellows' affection.

A farewell supper was given in his honour last night by his tutor, and that worthy man's voice actually trembled when he rose to wish him "Good-bye," in a neat speech, wherein he said "that they were going to part with one whom they all loved." ("Hear! hear!" from the boys.) He would not like to say that Wynyard had never given him any trouble by always doing his lessons properly (laughter and cheers); but one thing he could say, and did say, that all his sins were of omission, from carelessness alone, that he had never done a mean or unkind action, and that he carried away with him the love and

good will of his companions and tutor.   He
would conclude by saying that Wynyard
was " Certamine præstans, amicitiâ fidelis!
and wishing him every happiness in life."

How the old walls did re-echo to the
cheers which greeted this speech!   Dick's
voice, as he rose and thanked them all for
drinking his health, was very husky; and
when the boys rose and, hand-in-hand, sang
the touching words—

> " Should auld acquaintance be forgot,
>   And never brought to min' ?
> Should auld acquaintance be forgot,
>   And days o'·auld lang syne ? "

he fairly broke down, and wept like a child.

Then they cheered again and again, and
all crowded round to shake him by the
hand, and wish him God-speed.   I am sure
there was a dimness in that usually grim
tutor's eye as he laid one hand on Wynyard's shoulder, and warmly grasped his
hand with the other.   Else why did he
nervously adjust his spectacles, and try,
but utterly fail, to look fierce and for-
bidding as he did so?

Nearly all the necessary farewells have been said, and leave taken of Mr. Satchell, that famous cricketer; of Mr. Browning, genial and best of companions, and a host of others; last, but not least, of the immortal "Joby," who, stowing away a sovereign from Dick in his capacious nether garments, offered him a bun and jam to soften their parting.

Then, has he not said adieu to portly Powell, and fair Miss Goodman of the boat-house, not forgetting the obsequious "Gaffar" and "Jumbo," best of coxswains; to smiling Harry Webber and his amiable sisters; to venerable Mr. Barnes, and our worthy old friend, Joseph Brown?

His "one look more" at the various places of interest in the dear old school has been taken so often, that Dick has to put off his packing until almost the very last day of the term.

All his goods and chattels, save the silver cups and his mother's portrait, he gives to the kindly old boy's-maid, accompanying the gift by a hearty kiss and his own photograph, which that good old soul preserves to this day as one of her greatest treasures.

The last morning arrives, and Dick goes to take leave of the old "Head," who presents him with a book, according to custom, with his name written on the fly-leaf, and shakes hands with him, wishing him farewell.

Walking away by the cloisters, he comes across Burton. That youth had rather avoided his cousin since the Eton and Harrow match, but Dick, never having suspected the least treachery, has not once noticed the fact.

He turns with Burton now, and they walk together through the "playing-fields" for the last time.

"By Jove! only an hour left to catch the train!" exclaims Burton, looking at his watch. "Good-bye, Dick; I suppose we shall meet again some day?"

"You must come down to High Wynyard in September — sure to be lots of partridges—and the madre will be glad to see you again. Good-bye, old fellow; give my love to Uncle George."

Left alone, Dick yawns a little, and, walking back through the cloisters and quadrangle, seats himself on the low wall for the last time.

Did visions of his triumphs by that same wall rise up before him — triumphs that will never come over again? Was he thinking—

> " Let fancy still my sense in Lethe steep ;
>   If it be thus to dream, then let me sleep ? "

I think so, for the bright young face is strangely grave when he looks up again at the old chapel for the last time.

Then he crosses over to Miss Gellatly's house, emerging presently, followed by servants carrying innumerable portman-teaux, which are hoisted on to the roof of a Windsor fly.

Dick jumps in; the door is shut. He

waves his hand as he is driven rapidly away to the station. He is to pass the night in London, and go down to High Wynyard the following day.

CHAPTER VIII.

" FACILIS DESCENSUS AVERNI."

" Eh, mon! but it's a broad, guid road,
That road that leads us to sin!
Whoe'er could once ha' supposed
That the De'il could tak' us all in?"

DICK, arriving at Fenton's Hotel, is somewhat surprised to learn that a Mr. Allison
is waiting to see him, and still further
astonished when, on that gentleman pre-
senting his credentials in the shape of a
letter from Lady Nora Wynyard, that
hastily written note informs him that scarlet
fever has broken out in the village of High
Wynyard, and his mother begs him not to
return home for the present in consequence.
Apartments had been engaged, the note
went on to say, for Mr. Allison and himself

in Paris, and the writer hoped he would enjoy himself, and that, when tired of Paris, he would travel about the continent wherever he felt inclined.

Ralph Allison, the bearer of Lady Nora's note, and the temporary mentor that good lady had selected for our youthful Telemachus, was a distant connection of the Wynyard family. Undoubtedly clever, Allison had taken a brilliant degree at Oxford, followed by a short career at the bar; but, finding hard reading not to his taste, he took to writing articles for magazines, and was suspected of having been the author of sundry witty, but bitter and sarcastic, articles in a popular periodical.

Allison had visited nearly every capital in Europe, and being a keen observer and consummate judge of character, had picked up much of that superficial knowledge of life which some affect to despise, but which in reality makes such an agreeable companion. Whether Lady Nora would have selected him as a companion for her darling boy had she known that he used his opportunities of travel to cultivate the acquaintance of most of the coulisses, and otherwise enjoy thoroughly that vie Bohême so attractive for a time to a young man, we do not pretend to say; but, if she did, assuredly she judged wisely, for can there be a greater mistake than trying to keep a boy from that stormy ocean of pleasure, into which the moment he becomes his own master he may plunge headlong, without experience?

Dick was charmed with the frank, easy manners of his new acquaintance, and they parted, having agreed to meet at Charing Cross Station and cross over to Paris the very same evening.

A valet had been engaged by Allison for his charge, and punctually that individual arrived at the station, with his new master, and bustled about to take tickets and bestow the impedimenta in the van with a professional energy that augured well for his employer's future comfort.

Allison leans back in the carriage and

lights a full-flavoured Cabana, offering one
to Dick, who accepts the gift with some
misgiving, inasmuch as this is his first
sacrifice to the goddess of nicotine. He is
agreeably surprised, however, to find that
the soothing weed produces no uncomfortable sensations, but, deeming " discretion
the better part of valour," prudently declines
the offer of a second.

They have a calm passage from Folke-
stone, and Dick is highly amused at
Boulogne to see that the luggage is carried
by the fish-wives of that gay seaport to the
accompaniment of much gesticulation, and
expletives, not altogether complimentary in
character, are bandied about with considerable freedom.

They arrive in Paris about six in the
morning, and drive off to the apartments
which had been secured for them in the
Rue d'Albe, leaving Dick's valet behind to
clear the luggage from the douane.

Our travellers do a good deal of sight-
seeing in the course of the day. They visit

the Louvre, and walk down the Rue de la Paix, looking in at the shop windows in that gay thoroughfare. Dick's purse feels heavy in his pocket, but is considerably lightened after visiting a few of those seductive emporiums.

In the afternoon they drive in the Bois, and then Allison, a gourmet of the first water, shows Dick how to order a dinner at the Maison Dorée.

That cheerful youth enjoys the delicate entrêmets, and gulps down his Sauterne with a gusto which delights his Gamaliel. Nor do the attentions which he pays impartially to the Sauterne and "Veuve Clicquot" prevent his sharing a bottle of Lafitte of '58 before coffee.

After that invigorating beverage and a chasse, Allison proposes an adjournment to the theatre, a motion which Dick highly approves of; and saying, "Carried by an overwhelming majority," he links his arm in his companion's, and they go off to see the incomparable "Judic" in the "Timbale d'Argent."

" Facilis descensus Averni!" What would
his immaculate Eton tutor have thought
could he have seen his former pupil at
supper after the theatre that night ?

Allison had bidden some of his old acquaintances in the *corps du théâtre* (nothing
loth) to supper in the Palais Royal; and
Dick is surprised, but pleasantly so, at the
freedom of manner of the French ladies.
Seated between two fascinating coryphées,
one of whom condescends to light him a
cigar, puffing it into a glow with her own
fair lips, whilst the other peri undisguisedly
expresses her admiration of his sunny chestnut hair and *beaux yeux*, Dick looks highly
pleased with his companions, and pledging
them in a brimming glass of champagne,
invites all the houris to go with him to the
races on the following Sunday.

The Rubicon is passed. Where are
thoughts of Eton and boyhood now?
" Quantum mutatus ab illo Achille." Can
that dishevelled youth be the bright young
cricketer of a week ago—the lad who wept
at leaving Eton only yesterday ?

Dick, walking up the Champs Elysées to his lodgings towards three in the morning, is positive that the moon—which he has hitherto regarded as a model of propriety—palpably winks at him in a strangely indecorous manner, and is pained and surprised at the obstinate behaviour of his latch-key, which persistently refuses to enter the keyhole.

CHAPTER IX.

EROS.

"Altho' thou maun ne'er be mine,
Altho' even hope is denied,
'Tis sweeter for thee despairing
Than aught in the world beside."

BURNS.

UNCLE TOM'S conduct about this period is the source of much concern to his old servant, and considerable amusement to his friends at the club.

Usually most indifferent as to outward adornment, Mr. Wynyard, during the last few weeks, has ordered no less than three new coats from his tailor, altered his collars to a more ·becoming shape, changed the sober colour of his cravats, adopted a highly ornamental scarf-pin, and generally behaved himself in an inexplicable way.

Ten days ago he shamefully abandoned a small black meerschaum pipe, which had been his constant companion for years, and took to smoking cigarettes, which he detests. Moreover, he frequently reads the newspapers upside down at the club, and walks up and down the room in a manner most irritating to the nerves of his friends.

This morning Mr. Wynyard announces, somewhat nervously, to his old servant, that he expects a pair of patent-leather boots, and desires that astonished retainer to varnish them when they arrive.

This is the last straw! "Patent-leather boots at our age!" thinks Adams, grimly. "Well, what next, I wonder! I'll be bound there's a woman at the bottom of it!" he exclaims, when he regains his own room.

That shrewd domestic is right. Alas! for the years that should have brought discretion. It is the old, old story; and Uncle

Tom is madly, hopelessly in love as the veriest griff of eighteen.

It happened in this wise: Mr. Wynyard had been bidden to one of those water-parties, of which there are so many at the end of a London season, and though abominating that particular form of entertainment, a want of something to do, the hot weather, or his fate, took him down to Maidenhead, and thence to Skindle's, where he joined his party to row up to Marlow.

Mr. Wynyard did not much affect the society of ladies, and rather held aloof when he was introduced to Mrs. Ainslie. Need we say that, woman-like, she longed the more keenly to make the conquest of that reserved, grizzled misogynist, and liked him none the less that he seemed to avoid her? Perhaps, accustomed to admiration from the male sex, she was piqued at his indifference to her charms. At any rate, Mr. Wynyard found himself, to his annoyance, alone in a boat with the fair widow, and then (he was certain not by his contrivance) they lost their party, from some unexplained cause, and had to return to London alone.

Before entering the train at Maidenhead Mr. Wynyard thought his companion an agreeable woman. By the time they reached London, the journey had somehow seemed to him shorter than when alone in the morning. Mrs. Ainslie was charming—moreover, very good looking—just the style he most admired, he said to himself.

"You will come and call on me soon," she had said to him, on getting into her brougham at the station. And Mr. Wynyard *had* called, more than once, each time becoming more firmly convinced that there was but one woman he had ever loved in the world, and that that woman was Helen Ainslie.

Look at him now, as he carefully studies in the glass the folding of a bright blue cravat. You would not recognize him as the Uncle Tom we met at Eton only a month ago. The grizzled beard and moustache have been trimmed, the hair cut close and scented, and the whole outer man is completely altered in appearance.

Mr. Wynyard is evidently nervous this morning. A caraffe and liqueur-glasses stand on the table, and he has apparently been trying

> " To keep his spirits up
> By pouring spirits down."

Moreover, he upsets half a scent-bottle on his pocket-handkerchief in his preoccupation. His thoughts are far away. He has determined to lay his heart and all his worldly possessions this morning at the feet of a woman of whom he knows nothing. Nothing, indeed! What does he care to know, but that he loves her madly, devotedly, and that he would lay down his life this moment if the sacrifice would give her pleasure; that he would rather have one kind smile from Helen Ainslie's eyes than all the mines of Golconda?

Uncle Tom looks sadly again in the glass at the wrinkles and crow's-feet on his weather-beaten old face, and reflects rather

grimly that there is no fool like an old fool.
Then he takes a slim umbrella from the
stand, with a slight blush pins a rose in his
coat, swallows hastily a liqueur-glass of
maraschino, and goes out into the street.

He walks at a rapid pace down Piccadilly
and through Clarges Street, but very slowly
as he gets into Curzon Street. And then,
why—except that love is proverbially blind
—should he pass by Mrs. Ainslie's door, as
if he did not know the number, or had no
intention of calling on that lady?

Even when he has summoned courage to
ring the bell and ask if Mrs. Ainslie is at
home, he feels just like a school-boy at the
dentist's door; half hopes that Mrs. Ainslie
is out, at the next moment dreading that
she may have given orders of " Not at
home."

Mrs. Ainslie is at home. Will he walk
upstairs? And Uncle Tom, clinging tena-
ciously to his hat, follows the footman into
the drawing-room.

Years afterwards he remembers that

drawing-room—the strong scent of the ste-
phanotis in the room, the china on the
velvet shelves, the dress that Mrs. Ainslie
wears—even to the pattern of the carpet.

When the footman has left the room
(having very unnecessarily re-arranged
every article on the table, as Uncle Tom
thinks), Mr. Wynyard hopes Mrs. Ainslie is
well. He had not seen her for so long (he
had called and seen that lady only yesterday). Yes, he is soon going out of town.
London is certainly very hot, and every one
wants a change sometimes.

Then he draws his chair nearer to hers,
and coughs rather nervously several times
without speaking.

Does she guess what he means to say?
I am sure she does, for, woman-like, she
avoids the subject next his heart, and talks
away (rather too fast to seem quite natural,
and not waiting for an answer) on the last
meet of the Coaching Club. Does he think
the Princess will go down to Hurlingham
on Saturday? How shocking that young

Raven should have run away with Mrs. Papillon! and does he know if Colonel Papillon means to sue for a divorce?

Mr. Wynyard has answered absently once or twice; but his replies were frightfully irrelevant, had she noticed them. But she has not, and is about to begin a fresh string of queries, when he raises his hand gently and stops her. Then, desperately smoothing his hat round and round with his hand, he says—

"Forgive my interrupting you, but I didn't come here this morning to talk to you of Colonel Papillon—though I know and like him well—or his guilty wife. I want to speak of a far pleasanter subject— about yourself. I know that we only met a month ago, but I feel as if I had known you for years. You will say that I am too old—old enough, perhaps, to be your father —when I ask you to be my wife. But I love you very dearly, and will try to make you happy if you can take me as I am. Mrs. Ainslie—Helen, do you think you can try?"

It has come at last, and she has heard him without interruption to the bitter end. Coquette though she be, Helen Ainslie is sorry now, for she realizes that what has been mere pastime to her, has proved all too serious to him. Turning her face away from him, she leans on the mantelpiece, and does not speak.

He mistakes her silence, and begins rather eagerly, "If you would wish to take time—— "

But she interrupts him at once. " No, no, that would not be fair to you. I thank you very much for thinking me worthy to be your wife—for I do feel it very sincerely —but it can never, never be ; and I should be very wrong to let you think that I could change by time, for I know I never shall. I shall always like you as a friend. Cannot you be Uncle Tom to me, and forget that you have asked me to be your wife? " And she comes close to him, and holds out her hand as she speaks.

Mr. Wynyard takes the hand gently. " I

am sorry that you cannot like me well enough to marry me—I hardly expected you could—but I shall always love you just the same. When an old tree is struck it takes longer to recover than a young one. I shall not say that I shall try to forget you, for I know I could not. Good-bye; we shall not meet again." And he raises the hand, and touches it reverently with his lips.

"Good-bye; don't think unkindly of me—— "

But Mr. Wynyard is already half-way down the stairs, and goes out into the street, striding fiercely along, to the amazement of passers-by, seeing nothing, hearing nothing, as he walks back to his chambers.

Arrived there, he sinks into a chair, burying his face in his hands, and mutters, "So that's all over." Then, starting up and ringing the bell, he says to his old servant who enters, "Pack all my things; we start for New York by the next Cunard steamer, and for Liverpool to-morrow morning."

"And the patent-leather boots?" demands that bewildered domestic.

"Damn the patent-leather boots! Throw them away; I don't want them."

Adams, busily engaged in packing that evening, delivers himself to his master's wardrobe as follows: "And so we ain't a-going to have a missus after all, aren't we? Ah, well! when we gets to our time o' life, the sex is best let alone, says I."

Perhaps Mr. Adams is right, but poor old Uncle Tom carries a heavy heart back to Chicago. There are more lines about the weary eyes, and his partner observes that his run home has not done Mr. Wynyard so much good after all.

CHAPTER X.

ROUGE PERD—ET COULEUR.

"O Roulette ! how tempting thy charms
Are alike to the young and the old !
We ne'er think how much it harms,
Whilst we rake in the glittering gold."

AFTER a fortnight's gaiety in Paris, Dick began to grow weary of that gay city, and proposed to Allison to move further afield. They accordingly took train for Brussels, and thence to Cologne, where they remained three days only, Dick wondering how the eleven thousand virgins, whose relics he visited, could have been so foolish as to reside in such an unsavoury town.

Then they got on board a Rhine steamer and went as far as Mayence, branching off from there to Metz and Strasburg, where they marvelled at the glorious old clock in the cathedral. A fortnight later, Mentor and Telemachus arrived in Frankfort, and the same evening drove up to the door of the Rose Hotel in Wiesbaden.

After a hasty dinner at that comfortable hostelry, Allison conducted his charge to the Kursaal; and they drink their coffee at a small table in the garden, listening to the strains of the lovely " Soldaten Lieder Waltz" which Strauss's band are performing to an appreciative audience. Then Allison proposes that they shall "just see what is going on inside before walking home to bed."

They enter the gorgeous *salons de jeu*. What a scene this modern pandemonium presents! A Maltese is carrying all before him. Not a sound is heard as the impassive croupier deals out the cards. Then comes a pause, followed by a slight buzz of interest and astonishment, as several rouleaux of napoleons are pushed across the table by means of a rake to the successful

Maltese—immediately suppressed, however, as the croupier, unmoved as the Sphynx, recommences to deal.

What a strange scene, indeed! Every nationality is here represented. Russian and Frenchman, Greek and Austrian, Englishman and Jew, jostle one another round the long table. It is curious to watch the emotions depicted on the various faces.

Here is a Russian princess, with a secretary by her side to mark the *série*; not a muscle of her face moving as she rakes in a mass of glittering pieces. Seated next to her is a Prussian Jew of enormous wealth, with dirty hands; on the forefinger of the right flashes a diamond ring of great value, as he puts down a napoleon nervously on the red, only to snatch it back again before the cards are dealt. There is a tall, pale Englishman, losing heavily. Rouleau after rouleau is swept away by the remorseless rake; but he is essentially *beau jouer*, and— except by an involuntary trembling of the fingers as he pushes an enormous stake on to *couleur*—no one could guess that a second ample fortune is rapidly going the way of its predecessor.

Allison, after watching the game attentively for some time, takes a card and a pin from an attendant, and sits down at the Trente et Quarante table; Wynyard, who does not understand the game, wandering off to the next room, where the goddess of Rouge et Noir holds her court. Dick throws a double Frederick on the red. The roulette-wheel goes round, and——

" Dix huit, rouge, pair, et manque," says the croupier, monotonously. His stake is doubled, and he leaves it on. Eight consecutive times does the red come up, and he is the winner of a hundred and twenty-eight double Fredericks.

" A la masse ? " inquires the croupier. Dick nods, and the next moment, " Trente et un, noir, impair, et passe," says the inexorable voice, and the whole is swept away.

" What a bore!" carelessly thinks Dick. '' But I must try and win it back, though ; '

and he takes a chair next the croupier, vacated by a fair-haired young Teuton, and enters fully into the fascination of the game. He plays with varying luck, and at twelve o'clock, when the tables closed, found himself a loser of some twenty napoleons.

Early the next morning, to the amusement of Allison, who refuses to move until he has finished his after-breakfast cigar, Dick hurries off to the Kursaal, and takes a seat immediately the tables are opened.

The fair-haired Prussian officer, whose chair he had taken the preceding evening, is his neighbour at the green table this morning, and Dick, glancing up, is shocked to notice the hard, worn expression on the handsome young face, and the hungry, wolfish glare in his eyes, as stake after stake is swept away by the inexorable croupier, calm and impassive as Mephistopheles compassing the ruin of Faust. But soon his own play engrosses his attention, and Dick looks no more at his neighbour.

Once he places a napoleon *en plein* on twenty-one. The wheel goes round; the croupier monotonously says, " Messieurs, faites vos jeux, rien ne va plus," and the ball stops opposite twenty-one.

Dick, putting out his hand mechanically to take his winnings, is surprised to find it covered by another, guiltless of soap, and covered with many doubtful-looking rings, and to hear a shrill female voice exclaim, " Non, non, monsieur, c'est à moi!" But the croupier glances warningly at the unblushing French woman, dauntlessly mendacious as Sapphira of old, and she shrinks guiltily away under the scrutiny of that cold official eye.

So engrossed in the game is Dick, that he plays until six o'clock, losing largely; then snatches a hasty dinner in the Kursaal dining-room—eating little, indeed, but drinking copious draughts of Johannisberger.

How cool and seductive is that Rhine wine to the palate! how pleasantly it goes down the gamester's parched throat! And little do we reck how it mounts to the brain, setting it on fire, exciting and burning the coolest heads.

Surely Lurline must have poured out a flagon of that amber-coloured liquid for her over-bold admirer before she swept angrily in, and bore him away.

Dick, when he returns to court the fickle goddess of Fortune, has all his wits about him, but he feels strangely excited, and there is a brightness in his eyes and a burning red spot on either cheek, which augur badly for his caution.

He plays on, until, taking out his note-case, he is somewhat startled to find that he has actually lost over eight hundred pounds, and that but one note of a hundred remains in the silk case his mother had worked for him. He changes this for napoleons, and in a few minutes all are swept away. Then he rises to find Allison, and the two leave the Kursaal to stroll back to their hotel.

As they pass the fish-pond by the fountains, a pistol-shot rings out sharp and clear in the still night. Allison guesses what it means, and is not surprised when, on running to the spot whence the sound comes, they find the young Prussian officer, whose losses Dick had witnessed in the morning, stone dead, shot through the head by his own hand.

Alas! Rudolph von Eberstein, most promising of young hussars, kindliest and best of boon-companions! Can those distorted features be those of the handsome youth of this morning? Cover them up reverently and tenderly. His own mother would scarce be able to recognize them now, with that hideous, gaping wound through the temple.

CHAPTER XI.

AT HIGH WYNYARD.

"The stately homes of England,
　　How beautiful they stand,
　Amidst their tall ancestral trees,
　　O'er all the pleasant land !
　The deer across their greensward bound,
　　Thro' shade and sunny gleam,
　And the swan glides past the with them sound
　　Of some rejoicing stream."

HEMANS.

A BRIGHT, sunny afternoon late in October, and a lady is pacing slowly up and down the old stone terrace at High Wynyard, an open letter in her hand, and a somewhat anxious expression on her still handsome face.

It is Lady Nora Wynyard, and she has some cause to feel anxious just now, for

that morning's post had brought a letter
from an old friend, which said that the
writer felt it "her duty" (why do old
friends invariably find it their "duty" to
communicate disagreeable tidings?) to let
her friend know of her son's doings at
Wiesbaden.

The letter somewhat exaggerated Dick's
losses at roulette, trusted that all the
reports of Mr. Wynyard's *fredaines* were
not true, and ended by cheerfully conveying
the impression to the anxious mother that
her son was travelling fast on the broad
road to ruin.

Lady Nora takes her accustomed walk
through the conservatories, but the Cape
jessamine seems to have lost its scent, the
poinsettias are not of their usual brilliant
hue; as for the chrysanthemums, surely
never was such a wretched show in the
houses before! She takes the obsequious
head gardener sharply to task, to the
astonishment of that gifted individual, who
communicates to his subordinates, after-

wards, that he " has never found miladi so contrary like before."

She goes back to the morning-room, but somehow her knitting-kneedles are mislaid, and when they are found the wool is altogether the wrong shade.

Feeling utterly miserable, womanlike, she indulges in a good cry and a cup of tea—that panacea for female woes—and then, strange to say (who can understand the varying moods of a woman?), she feels better. After all, the letter may have exaggerated. Mrs. Bidwell always made the worst of everything; and, as she looks out of the window and sees the old clergyman of the village coming up the avenue on his sturdy cob, Lady Nora thinks she will confide in her old friend, and feels relieved at the prospect.

That worthy pastor, coming slowly up the avenue of beech trees, thinks he has never seen the old house look more beautiful. And, indeed, the view is very lovely.

Built of Portland stone, in the reign of

Stephen, as a monastery, but now faced
with red brick of a deep dull colour, High
Wynyard still retains much of the original
character of the priory. The old chapel,
overgrown with ivy, still stands on the east
side, though now it forms one of a suite of
reception-rooms running the whole length
of the house. A banqueting-hall, added in
the reign of Charles II., with large mul-
lioned windows, faces the south. The
entrance is on the east side, under an old
archway, above which is a quaint clock.
All the windows on this side are oriel in
shape, and of stained glass, with the ar-
morial bearings of Vavasour, Curwen, Be-
lasyse, and De Roos. Over the hall door
are the arms of the Wynyard family, and
their motto, graven in old English cha-
acters—

> " Let Wynyarde holde
> That Wynyarde hath,"

surmounted by the royal arms.

The flower-garden is on the south side of
the house ; and on the west, four terraces,

one below another, lead to an old bowling-
green, whence a lawn slopes gradually down
to the river Thames. The park round
three sides of the house is well planted
with clumps of magnificent old trees,
amongst which the graceful deer wander.
The south lodge opens into a long avenue
of gigantic oaks, throwing out their huge
naked arms like deformed giants.

Mr. Preston, the clergyman, on his first
arrival in the parish, had asked the old
bailiff, "Which Wynyard was supposed to
have planted these grand old trees?"

"Planted!" had replied that aged ser-
vitor, indignantly; "they were never
planted; they are as old as the world!"

But we are keeping good Mr. Preston
waiting at the hall door, and, though the
sun is bright, there is a chill east wind—as
that worthy divine thinks, ringing the bell
louldly a second time.

The grey-haired butler opens the door,
and Mr. Preston walks into the fine old
hall, panelled with oak black with age.

On the walls are hung ancient weapons of
warfare, spears from Abyssinia, chain armour
from the Holy Land, Greek daggers, and
Afghan shields, buffalo heads, and the horn
of a rhinoceros.   Over the huge open fireplace are two crossed cavalry swords which
had belonged to Captain Wynyard, Dick's
father.

The butler fancies " that her ladyship is
in her boudoir," so the clergyman is conducted up the broad black oak staircase,
adorned with quaintly carved figures, and
up which (except for the broad shallow
steps) a coach and four might conveniently
be driven by a skilful whip.   At the first
landing the staircase branches right and
left, leading to an open gallery, which runs
round the hall, and out of which open the
principal bedrooms and Lady Nora's own
sitting-room.

That lady is not in her room, however, so
they descend to the old picture-gallery.   It
is a splendid old room, lighted by three
large oriel windows, the tops of which are

of stained glass, and blazoned with the
arms of the Villiers and Scortons, Stapyl-
ton and Fairfax, quartered. The centre
window has a Saracen's head rising out of
a crown—the crest given to Sir Miles de
Wynyarde by the King of England, for
slaying a Saracen in single combat before
himself and the King of France; and the
combat is depicted on the window below
the crest.

There, amongst a long line of ancestral
portraits, is the picture of Sir Miles de
Wynyarde—that lean, wiry-looking man on
horseback. A battle is raging (apparently
under his horse's legs), and a turbaned de-
fender of the faith is writhing under the
quadruped's hoofs; but, perfectly unmoved
by his somewhat "warm" position, Sir
Miles is waving his hand blandly in the
direction of a tower in the distance.

Here is Sir Egbert de Wynyarde, knight
and high sheriff of Oxfordshire in the time
of good Queen Bess; and there, in violet
velvet coat and lace ruffles, is the first

baronet, Sir Bryan Wynyard, simpering under a powdered wig.

What a lovely face is this girl's near the fireplace! Ah, there is a sad story attached to that picture. It is the portrait of Dorothy Wynyard, who was wrongfully suspected of having become a mother before she was a wife. Her brother, Sir Giles Wynyard (through the treachery of a servant), discovered his sister's secret, and suspected his younger brother's tutor to be her lover. Mad with rage at the (as he thought) dishonour cast on his old name, the story goes that Sir Giles burst into Dorothy's bedroom about midnight, awoke his terrified sister, and, producing two dice in a silver cup, forced her, nearly fainting with fright, to cast for the life of either her child or her lover. Sir Giles threw sixes. With a fearful shriek that resounded through the old house, Dorothy, clinging to her brother's knees, and imploring him to forgive her, fainted from terror. After that night she never recovered her reason, and was confined to the one room in charge of an old nurse; and the servants declare to this day that in Queen Anne's room, on one night in the year, is heard the tramp of a heavy boot, followed by the wail of an infant and a scream from a woman's voice. The silver cup has been handed down as an heirloom, and figures on the tall mantelpiece at one end of the gallery.

Retribution does not appear to have overtaken Sir Giles, for he entertained King Charles II. on his way from Oxford to Windsor, and was appointed Receiver-General by the merry monarch. But perhaps the sins of the father were visited on the son, for Sir Hugh Wynyard had no children, and the baronetcy became extinct, the estates passing to his sister's son, who took the name of Wynyard.

That is the portrait of Sir Giles, between the windows—the stern, hard-looking, beetle-browed man in the scarlet coat—and—— Is it fancy, or is there a broad red stain across the face, cast by the stained glass in the window?

Along the wall are the portraits of Sir Cuthbert Wynyard in the dress of an admiral in the time of James I.; of Richard Wynyard in blue coat and brass buttons, with his long hair gathered into a pigtail behind. Next to him is the portrait of Dick's grandfather, Godfrey Wynyard, on horseback; and over the low doorway hangs the likeness of a young man in the uniform of a lancer. It is Captain Wynyard, Dick's father. There is little resemblance to be traced to his son, and a slightly mocking expression about the grey eyes gives a cynical look to the otherwise handsome face, contrasting with the affectionate look in the blue eyes of Lady Nora, who, in bridal dress, is next to her husband's portrait on the wall.

That lady is writing in the adjoining room as the clergyman opens the door, and, looking up on his entrance, says, " Oh, how do you do, Mr. Preston? You are just in time for a cup of tea, and I have so much to talk to you about."

And then why—when she is burning to consult him about Dick's peccadilloes—does she energetically discuss the prospects of the village coal club, and ask if Jim Rabbits has received his deserts for poaching, and whether there are likely to be many pheasants in the home coverts this year?

Perhaps she is doing penance for her thoughtless son's misdeeds. Perhaps it is because she is a thorough woman, and could not go straight to the point, however near her heart that point may be.

At last, however, an inquiry from Mr. Preston after Dick leads up to that youth's misdeeds, and Lady Nora pours out her woes and misgivings to her old friend.

That worthy man crosses his legs, one thumb and forefinger steal into his waistcoat-pocket, the other hand strokes his well-shorn chin reflectively, whilst he listens to the incriminating letter being read out.

"Well, you see, my dear lady," he says,

after listening attentively, " circumstances alter cases. Boys will be boys, all the world over, you know; and Dick will be his own master in a year or so, so it is of no use interfering with him now. Far better let him buy his own experience. We all have to do it. How uncommonly wise youngsters would be if they only listened to the experiences of their elders! Too wise, perhaps!" and Mr. Preston chuckles at his little joke. " Now, my dear good lady, do be persuaded by me, and let the boy alone. You can't keep him always tied to your apron-strings, you know. So say nothing to him about this letter, and let him go his own way. I know Dick too well to think he would do anything really dishonourable."

" You have taken a load off my mind. I am always so glad to have your advice."

" Ha, ha!" laughed Mr. Preston cheerily, " I wish all my parishioners were of the same opinion. What work I have, to be sure, with that silly Jane Spriggs, who will put blue ribbons in a pink bonnet, and run

after that good-for-nothing young Tom
Loafer. Won't listen to a word I say,
I assure you, or her foolish mother either.
But I must be off," said the worthy divine,
taking out his watch.

"Good-bye. Thank you ever so much
for your kind advice. Another cup of tea
before you go."

"Not another drop, my dear madam.
Good-bye." And Mr. Preston takes his
hat and makes his way to the hall. In a
few minutes he is jogging briskly down the
avenue on his sturdy old cob.

CHAPTER XII.

PER MARE, PER TERRAS.

"When I was at home I was in a better place;
  But travellers must be content."
                                SHAKESPEARE.

AFTER poor Von Eberstein's violent death roulette completely lost its charm for Dick Wynyard. Allison, indeed, continued to woo the fickle goddess. Why should the death of a man he didn't even know prevent his playing? he asked; and added (brutally, as it seemed to Dick), Besides, it showed such a want of *savoir-vivre* to die when he was not obliged to.

They remained ten days longer at Wiesbaden; but although Allison took his seat daily at the tables, Dick never went near the Kursaal again, making lonely excursions on the Rhine (once, indeed, he went over to Homburg, but only for the day), until he began to feel very much bored, and to think that foreign travel was not so amusing or improving after all.

Perhaps perceiving this, or perhaps having lost as much at Trente et Quarante as he deemed it prudent to risk, Allison proposed to his charge that they should move on to "fresh fields and pastures new" —a proposition which Dick eagerly assented to, and the following evening saw them starting for Hamburg, thence to take steamer for Copenhagen. Mentor and Telemachus stayed a week in Copenhagen, and at the end of it both were of opinion that the capital of Denmark was about the dullest city that two wandering Englishmen could be condemned to visit. Allison, after spending a long, wearisome evening in the Tivoli Gardens, exclaimed, "Oh, Dick, I shall have to take to teaching you Greek in self-defence, if we stay much longer in this dull, virtuous city. I feel that 'Othello's occupation's gone.' Let us go round by sea to Stockholm. It is a charming place in summer, and in this hot weather the sea will be delightful."

"By all means," replied that youth, thinking that if Othello's usual occupations were at all like his friend's, that swarthy warrior must have been far more addicted to gambling than Desdemona could altogether have approved of. " Let us leave Copenhagen to-morrow, if you like. Will you find out all about the boat? Give us a light, will you? Even my cigar seems bored 'to extinction,' and has gone out."

" We were to have gone to Elsinore to-morrow, you know ; but I dare say Elsinore won't miss us much, so we will strike that out of the programme."

"Oh yes! I don't care the least to see Hamlet's grave, so that motion stands adjourned *sine die*."

They find a boat starting the following

afternoon, and after a three days' voyage along the coast, are about fifteen miles from Stockholm, when the steamer breaks down, and they have to be towed in by a tug, amid most lovely scenery and groups of islands, arriving about sunset.   Dick, standing in the bows of the vessel, thinks it is a glorious view spread out before him, and sees with wonder that Stockholm is built on three islands, the streets rising one above the other in the distance, with the handsome palace in the background.

Notwithstanding Allison's favourable report of Stockholm, the pair do not find much to amuse themselves with, and Dick gives it as his opinion that "a fellow can't live or amuse himself long on only scenery," and soon they are again on the wing.   They leave Stockholm in the early morning in a steamer, and touch at Abo, in Finland, and then at Helsingfors, where Dick drives in a Russian drosky for the first time, in company with an American whose acquaintance he had formed on board the *Dagmar*, Allison following with Mr. Flake's handsome spouse.

Leaning against the bulwarks the next evening, Dick, whilst smoking his post-prandial cigar, admires a little terrier that is curled up comfortably on Mr. Flake's knees.

"Ah, sir!" said Mr. Flake, "you wouldn't guess it, maybe, but that there leetle dawg has stood me in over thirty yellow-boys already."

"Why, how's that?" inquired Dick, thinking to himself that thirty pounds does seem rather an excessive price for such a diminutive animal.

"Wal, I promised my wife that I wouldn't let on to any one about it; but the fact is, sir, between ourselves, Mrs. F. is uncommon sweet on that there quadruped. Wal, last night, after we had retired to our downies, that cussed leetle hound he begins to pant, and then to howl most dismal. 'Jump up, Cornelius,' says Mrs. F., 'and give the poor crittur something to wet his whistle.' 'Snakes!' says I; but up I jumped, and found a tumbler all handy, and, kinder lucky, with water in it too, sir, and I giv' it 'Stripes' to drink. He lapped a bit, he did, and then I chucked the remains out o' winder into the briny. We were goin' smooth at the time, sir, and somehow the splash *did* sound kinder *loud* for only a leetle water, which I remarked it to Mrs. F. 'What did you give him the water in?' says she. 'In the tumbler, my love,' says I, when she giv' a kinder dismal screech; and what do you think I'd bin and gone and done, sir? Why, that tarnation loud splash I'd heard was Mrs. F's. best set of teeth, and there was three and twenty yellow-boys a gone coon; so now you see how that there leetle dawg has stood me in thirty quid. Mrs. F. she won't appear on deck no more now she's lost her fixings, and I'll bet my pile to a cocktail, I don't hear the last of those darned teeth just yet awhile. Good night, gentlemen all;" and Mr. Flake walked solemnly away, carrying the little dog "Stripes" in his arms, leaving Dick and Allison convulsed with laughter.

They see no more of Mr. or Mrs. Flake on reaching St. Petersburg, when they get into a drosky, and are driven at a terrific pace over the wooden bridge of the Neva, down the Nevskoi Perspective to Demuth's Hotel, where a gigantic chasseur (clad in furs, notwithstanding the heat) received them, and carried off their passports to the police-station. Allison and his charge do a great deal of sight-seeing in St. Petersburg. They visit the Taurida Palace, and marvel at the splendid ball-room, which is said to be half a mile in circumference, and the winter garden, running the whole length of the palace, roofed in and, though divided by marble pillars, forming part of the ball-room. Then they go on to the winter palace, considered, deservedly, the most splendid royal palace in the world, and the hermitage adjoining, built by the great Empress Catherine, with its magnificent collection of paintings, and rooms filled with jewels and objects of vertu. Last, but not least, the museum of Peter the Great, where they see the tools and various manufactures of that extraordinary man.

They spend a pleasant afternoon wandering about the gardens of Peterhof, watching the wonderful fountains play, and take train to Tsarko-Seloe, most charming of summer retreats.

Nor do they neglect altogether to improve the shining hour by a wholesome course of instruction, for they go out to Kronstadt, where part of the Russian fleet lie at anchor, and are shown over those grim vessels.

The streets do not amuse our friends so much, for they continually lose their way if they walk about much. "And no wonder," observed Dick; "for how can one read the name of a street when the printing looks like Greek written backwards? and nobody seems to speak any intelligible language except German, which I don't understand."

Perhaps the reason why Russians are

almost invariably good linguists, may be that their own language is so difficult to read and pronounce, that other tongues are comparatively easy to them.

CHAPTER XIII.

AT VIENNA.

" Oh, there flows swift the Danube blue—
A rushing, roaring river."

" WE'LL go back by another route, Dick,"
said Allison one morning, after carefully
surveying an atlas. " Let us take steamer
to Stettin, in Pomerania, and get down from
there to Berlin."

" All right," returned that youth, somewhat inarticulately—in the act of shaving
his chin and cheeks, carefully avoiding the
upper lip, where a promising moustache has
begun to make its appearance. " We'll
finish off with another theatre to-night."

Accordingly, Allison ascertains with some
difficulty that there is a boat, though not
a passenger-boat, sailing for Stettin, and

that the skipper (for a consideration) will land them on the coast of Pomerania.

They accordingly embark, and float down the Neva, past Peterhof and grimly frowning Kronstadt, out into the Baltic Sea. They are astonished about ten o'clock that night to see the northern moon, of a dull orange colour, looking to be only a few hundred yards from the ship, but still more astonished at the inconsiderate want of care shown by a Russian frigate, apparently practising their guns—for a ball, and another, plough up the sea at a very short distance astern of the vessel.

Mentioning this uncomfortable fact to the old German skipper, that worthy, without removing his cherished pipe from his mouth, says deliberately, with a grin, "Ja, ja. I hab a large cargo von tabak mit me, and I forget to bay duty. Das ist one revenue vessel. I sink zey schniff zee tabak ist nod baid for, and zey cannon bang to signal schtop. But I nod schtop. No, nod ad all. Goot-bye, mein lieber freund," he adds, sarcastically waving his pipe at the Russian frigate, which they are rapidly distancing.

"What an unmitigated, smuggling old ruffian it is!" says Dick to Allison; "but I like the old beggar for his pluck, though."

They are landed at Stettin, however, without any mishap, and after strolling through the old town, purchase some curiously carved wooden pipes, ornamented with huge tassels; and then they take train for Berlin, where they go to the Hôtel de Rome. Both dislike Berlin,—just like a huge camp of soldiers,—and, after sitting one morning "Unter den Linde," they leave for Dresden, where they look at the china and capital collection of pictures, and so down to Vienna, where our travellers arrive late at night, driving to the Archduke Charles.

Vienna—one of the most fascinating of capitals!—how can we do justice to all your charms,—to the Prater, those lovely Lichtenstein Gardens, the colossal Theatre au der Wien, and, last but not least, those amusing, never-to-be-forgotten balls in the Volksgarten?   Where do we ever hear such music now, as we heard there in our youth, when Plancus was consul?   Strauss surpasses himself at Vienna.   Do we ever dance now as we valsed in those days, to the notes of " Neue Wien," " Morgenblätter," or " Casino Tanze "?

Ah! Frederick R——, you are a reverend dean now, and a pillar of the Church.   Perhaps some day you may be a bishop, though you do walk so solemnly about with a sort of " Nolo-episcopari " look on your reverend countenance, which deceives no one but yourself and that wife whom you keep in such truly admirable subjection.   Have you ever told her of those days of your youth at Vienna—of those excursions to Schönbrunn?

And Bertie S——, crack cotillon leader though you afterwards became, if you ever read these lines, will you tell me if you ever enjoyed any like those roystering dances of yore, in the Volksgarten?

" Eheu fugaces anni labuntur ! " I fear we might be more critical now, as the years have glided swiftly away, bringing experience in their train !

Dick and Allison thoroughly enjoy Vienna ; the latter had visited it before, and made a most agreeable cicerone. He looked up his fair acquaintances, accompanied by some of whom he and Dick made excursions to Maüerbach and Steinbach, the latter playing the part of Amphitryon with great glee at suppers to these Meniads.

But all pleasures must have an end, and as the winter came on Allison urged that they should go south. Accordingly they left Vienna, with regret, for Munich—coldest of cities—passed over the Brenner, through the Tyrol, to Innsprück, and arrived at Verona. Thence they travelled on to Venice, Dick hugely enjoying the novelty of a gondola ; but, as it rained every day during their stay, both were glad to go on to pleasant Milan, with its glorious cathedral looking like lace-work in the moonlight, and that wonderful, dreadful statue of "L'homme pellé" (figure of a man with the whole skin of his body flying over the shoulder).   Thence they go to sirocco-haunted Turin, to gloomy Bologna, and so down to Florence—sunny, gay, delightful Florence!

Allison had written for apartments before leaving Venice, and had secured some look-ing out over the Arno, not very far from the Cascine.

They dine within an hour of their arrival, and Dick thoroughly appreciates the cuisine and the excellent "pomard" provided; but he finds time to observe that Allison does not eat with his usual appetite, and when that cool-headed gentleman sends away un-tasted a salmi de becassines, Dick is loud in his regret and astonishment.

"Why, what can be the matter with you, Allison, not to try that? You seem to be altogether off your feed to-night. What is it?"

"Oh no, there is nothing the matter but

my own thoughts. Very few of us can afford to look back, you know; and I was remembering that the last time I was in Florence, poor Charles L—— dined with me in these very rooms, and sat just where you are now. What a cheery, genial companion he was, to be sure! Such a fund of anecdote : seldom dull. And then, what a judge of character! I recollect, on the occasion I speak of, poor L—— and I had been talking about the wonderful difference that steam had made in civilization, and he recited a song which he had composed about the trains, and called the 'Song of the Stoker.' Wonderfully clever it was, to be sure; and, I remember, made quite an impression on my mind of the genius that could sit down and write off a song on any given subject like that."

"Oh, do sing it to me," interrupted Dick. "I wish the old days of stage-coaches were back myself, though perhaps they were rather slow."

"I am not sure that I can remember it

now; but hand me a cigar, and ring the bell for coffee, and I will try." And Allison began—

"THE SONG OF THE STOKER.

" Rake, rake, rake,
     Ashes, cinders, and coal ;
   The fire we make
   Must never slake,
     Like the fire that roasts a soul.

" Hurrah ! my boys, 'tis a glorious noise,
     To list to the stormy main ;
   But no wave-lashed shore,
   Nor lion's roar,
     Ever equalled an express train.

" 'Neath the burning sun our course we run,
     No water to slake our thirst ;
   Nor ever a pool
   Our tongue to cool,
     Except the boiler burst.

" The courser fast, the trumpet's blast,
     Sigh after us in vain ;
   And even the wind
   We leave behind,
     With the speed of a special train.

" A mile a minute, on we go—
     Hurrah for my courser fast !
   His coal-black mane,
   And his fiery train,
     And his breath—a fiery blast.

"On and on, till the day is gone,
  We rush with a goblin scream ;
And the cities at night,
They start with affright
  At the cry of escaping steam.

"Bang ! bang ! bang !
  Shake, shiver, and throb ;
The sound of our feet
Is the piston's beat,
  And the opening valve our sob !

"Our Union-jack is the smoke-train black,
  That thick from the funnel rolls ;
And our bounding bark
Is a gloomy ark,
  And our cargo—human souls.

"Rake, rake, rake,
  Ashes, cinders, and coal ;
The fire we make
Must never slake,
  Like the fire that roasts a soul."

" Capital ! " exclaimed Dick. " By Jove !
that is good—

'The fire we make
Must never slake,
  Like the fire that roasts a soul.'

He must have been clever."

"Indeed, you would have said so had you
heard him recite it himself before he went
to Trieste. I never saw him again. I am

afraid, too, I have forgotten part of it; but that gives the idea."

"I should think so! Excellent! You must try and write it out for me to keep."

"Well, I feel rather sleepy, and shall turn in early to-night. Good night, Dick; breakfast any time you like in the morning."

Dick smokes another cigar, and then dozes in his chair, waking up with a start to find the fire gone out, and the clock pointing to a quarter-past two.

CHAPTER XIV.

HORACE AUDLEY.

" Ladye, he is dead and gone !
Ladye, he's dead and gone !
And at hys head a greene grasse turfe,
And at hys heels a stone."

Percy Reliques.

FLORENCE as it was—the capital before Victor Emmanuel occupied Rome—was indeed a city of pleasure, as Wynyard and Allison soon found. Provided with letters of introduction, the two Englishmen were invited everywhere. Dick started a team, which he drove on the Cascine in the afternoons, to the admiration of fair—and the envy of male—Florence.

The fair Florentines admired Dick immensely, and were not backward in letting him know the fact, to the amusement of Allison, who laughingly accused him of having become a Millamour of the deepest dye. To do him justice, Dick was perfectly impartial in his attentions, and perhaps they liked him none the less on that account, when no one could be said to be the favourite in the field. Nothing could storm Allison's heart, which might have been of adamant, so impervious was he to female charms. And, indeed, he had a cynical way of treating women, which, while it made them fear him, was not so attractive as the careless grace of Dick's manner.

Ball succeeded ball. Shooting-parties in the Maremna and the adjoining country gave place to the Carnival—that strange festival in which the Italians so delight, and into the spirit of which Dick entered with a zest that amused his more experienced companion.

But all things must come to an end; and, after countless adieux (at some of which

tears fell thickly as the leaves at Vallam-
brosa), our travellers found themselves in
Rome—dear, dirty old Rome.

After gay Florence, Rome (for this was
in the days when the Papal court still
flourished) seemed deserted and dull. The
Pincian Hill was a poor exchange for the
crowded Cascine; the Piazza di Spagnia
dirty and oppressive, compared to the Lung'
Arno. How muddy and slow seemed the
Tiber, after the swiftly rushing Arno!

Allison and Dick felt the change, and
though they presented their letters of introduction and went to a few balls, the air of
Rome seemed heavy and relaxing, and both
were very glad to go on to Naples, where
they took charming apartments on the
Chiaja; and Dick chartered a yacht (which
Allison christened the *Nora*), in which they
made excursions about the coast, and over
to Capri and Sicily, being especially charmed
with sunny Palermo. When on shore the
yacht was moored down by Santa Lucia,
and they drove over to Pompeii and Hercu-

laneum, Allison being greatly interested in the ancient frescoes at Pompeii.

Sitting one afternoon in the gardens of the Villa Réale, listening to the band, Dick noticed a young Englishman seated in a Bath-chair, and was shocked to find that the attenuated features and powerless limbs belonged to one Horace Audley, whom he had known as one of the best fives players, and captain of his house at Eton.

Dick went up and shook hands with his old friend, and it wrung his honest heart to hear that Audley had been pronounced, by a conclave of doctors in London, to be in a deep decline, and they had sent him out to pass the winter at Naples, in the hope that the warm air of the sunny south might benefit his chest. But, indeed, to look at his pale, shrunken features, unnaturally large eyes, and thin, almost transparent hands, it was evident that the fell destroyer had affixed his seal on the forehead here; and Audley said as much sadly to Dick, begging him to come and sit with him sometimes.

"I do feel so lonely out here with only a servant near me," the invalid had said. And Dick had promised to go.

Indeed, after that afternoon in the Villa Réale, he never allowed a day to pass without visiting Audley. Even Allison was touched by the invalid's helplessness and resignation to suffering, and often cheered him with his amusing anecdotes and clever cynical remarks on man—and especially woman—kind.

As Dick and Allison walked down the Chiaja of a morning, they used to see Horace Audley's pale face wistfully watching at the window to catch a glimpse of them as they went by; and many a time, when bent on some expedition, did they turn back, haunted by the wistful eyes of the invalid, and pass the day by his chair instead.

As the spring came on, Audley evidently grew weaker and weaker day by day, and in April his appearance alarmed Dick, who begged of him to return to England. Ac-

cordingly, one brilliant day in April, the
trio started from Naples, intending to travel
by very easy stages, on account of the invalid, to London.

They got gradually to Milan, and thence
to Como and Bellaggio—delightful, charming Bellaggio.   Here Audley, who had
hitherto borne the journeys badly, rallied
amazingly, to the relief of his companions;
and many were the excursions they made
on the lovely Lake of Como, Audley steering,
wrapped in shawls, amidst a pile of soft
cushions—Dick and Allison rowing gently
along, halting to look at Villa d'Este, and
pointing out places of interest to the
invalid.

After a fortnight at Bellaggio, they went
on to Chiavenna, and made the ascent
slowly to the top of the Splügen, rested
there a night, and started the following
morning en route for Coïre.

They had made half the descent, during
which Audley had been in capital spirits,
when a blinding snowstorm came on sud-

denly. They hurried on as fast as possible, went at a gallop down the Via Mala; but by the time they reached Coïre, Audley was chilled and coughing painfully. They put him to bed immediately, but to no avail; by the next morning it was evident to all that he was sinking fast, and he himself was aware of the sad fact.

He sent for Dick that evening, and, taking his hand, said, " Sit down close to me, Dick, dear old man. I know I am going fast, and I have something to say to you first."

"Oh no, no; don't say that, Audley. You will beat the doctors yet. We shall see you strong again some day."

"No, no, Dick; I know better. Listen. I have not much to say, or to leave behind me. The estate is entailed, and goes to my brother. He is strong, and will do better with the old place than I could, perhaps. Besides him, I have hardly a relation in the world. My father, you know, was a hard, cold, unsympathetic man. He is dead

now, poor old fellow; but I remember
how he used to delight in opening all the
doors and windows, more especially if any
one was ailing.   I wonder if he would
like to be here now, to open that window
on me," said Audley, with a sad smile that
wrung the heart of the listener, who could
only sob convulsively and press the other's
hand.

Audley went on—" When I was last here,
Dick, on my way to Italy, I wandered about
the place, and went into the little cemetery
across the stream.   I should like you to
bury me—there, in ' God's-acre.'   What a
pretty word that is the Germans use, Dick,
—' God's-acre.'   Only a plain cross, Dick,
with these words, ' Trustie to the end.'
Something to drink—quick!   I—feel worse
—and I must—say more.   Ah, thanks; now
I feel better.   This thick gold ring I want
buried with me, and a locket—with hair
you will find on a—chain round my—neck.
I am going—going fast now, Dick.   How I
—seem to see the dear old—school at Eton

—once—more. Good-bye, dear old—fellow.
Good-bye—Daisy, my—darling.''

*   *   *   *   *

" Only a woman's hair," wrote Dean
Swift, on a love-token. What stories and
romances might not be woven from an old
glove, a faded flower, a lock of hair, if one
should find one of these relics " years
after " !

Dick never knew the history of that
locket and ring which he buried reverently
with his dead friend. He and Allison followed in the funeral cortége that wended
its sad way slowly one morning to the little
cemetery across the stream, where a small
white cross, inscribed—

𝔗𝔬 𝔱𝔥𝔢 𝔐𝔢𝔪𝔬𝔯𝔶 𝔬𝔣

HORACE CHARLES AUDLEY,

Died 18—,   aged 23 Years.

" Trustie to the end."

marks his last resting-place on earth, and
the cool summer breezes from the Alps blow
softly over the flowers on the grave of poor
Horace Audley.

CHAPTER XV.

HOMEWARD BOUND.

"Such is the patriot's boast where'er we roam—
The first, best country ever is at home."

GOLDSMITH.

AFTER the sad event recorded in the last chapter, there remained no object to take Wynyard and Allison at once homewards; so they accordingly, after leaving Coïre, branched off at Basle to Lucerne, where they spent a pleasant fortnight, and then proceeded gradually to Berne [and Vevay, thence to Lausanne, and stayed for some time at the Hôtel Beau Rivage, at Ouchy, on the delightful Lake of Geneva. Here the time passed very pleasantly and rapidly away. Bathing, sailing on the lake, with occasional excursions over to Évian-les-Bains in Savoy, Vevay, or Geneva, principally occupied them, until both were surprised to find that August had come so quickly upon them.

Returning late one night to Ouchy, after dining in Lausanne, Allison and Wynyard, as they were descending the stone "rampe" leading from the town, saw a rather noisy group of Swiss surrounding a man who was lying on the ground, and apparently incapable, so far as they could see by the dim light, of raising himself unaided.

"What is it, I wonder?" said Dick, carelessly.

"Oh, only some 'braves Suisses' rather more 'braves' than usual, after a debauch on Yvorne, I should think."

But at this moment the prostrate man, hearing voices, most unmistakably sang out, "Help! help!" loudly.

"By Jove! it's an Englishman, I do believe," exclaimed Dick. "Come on, Allison." And with a few well-directed blows

Allison and Dick soon succeeded in scattering the group of Swiss, and raised the fallen man.

On propping him up against a lamp-post, they discovered that he was not much hurt, only shaken and bruised a little by his fall on the stones, while there was but one cut on his cheek from a stick. As he turned his head for the first time to thank them for their timely aid, Allison exclaimed, " Why, good heavens ! it must be Jim Padmore. Why, what ill wind has blown you to Lausanne, of all places, my man ? "

" Mr. Allison ! I thought as I knowed your voice, sir," said their protégé, stroking his bullet-head ; and then, evading Allison's direct question, he continued, " Well, you see, sir, I had bin a-playin' cards with them Swiss chaps—reg'lar duffers they was, too, —at a caffy, and I won their money, which made them a bit sore like ; they was half tight, too, afore we left the caffy, and they sets on me a-comin' down this place, which you come up and perwented them, thank you, gentlemen both. I've bin a-waitin' to get back to England for some time, on'y the needful is scarce with me, gents."

"Well, here's my card," interrupted Dick. "I am staying at the Beau Rivage at present, and if you want assistance for your journey, come and ask for me there."

"Thank you, sir. Much obliged, I'm sure," said Mr. Padmore, touching his hat. "Good night, sir; good night, Mr. Allison;" and he quickly vanished back towards Lausanne.

"Been playing at the Café du Grand Pont, and our precious friend probably cheated the Swiss at cards, I should think. 'Hinc illæ lachrymæ,'" said Allison, as they strolled on after their brief adventure. "Most awful scamp, that fellow Padmore, Dick. I wonder how he got here to Lausanne, of all places. He never told us that, by-the-by."

"Oh, I remember he seemed to recognize you. What do you know about him?"

"Well, I think I know a great deal about

him, and not much good either. But it would bore you to hear it."

"Not the least. I am rather interested in the fellow. He has a sharp face; so fire ahead."

"Well," said Allison, "the first time I ever met him was about seven years ago, at Newmarket, when he was rough-rider in a training stable; and then, as he was sharp, he was promoted afterwards to be a sort of under-trainer in the same stable, but got sent away for something or other, and I lost sight of him for a year or so. Then, one day I met him in Scarborough, with three fat, apoplectic-looking Blenheim spaniels, which he was tugging along by a cord, much against their will. I stopped, and asked him what he was doing; and the impudent rascal told me he had turned 'dog-doctor,' and that the three obese canine specimens with him belonged to an old maiden lady at Harrogate, who had consulted him once about a pet Blenheim spaniel, which she had stuffed with chicken and gravies to repletion, and allowed to lay on a cushion before the fire without any exercise whatever. He then told me, with a cunning leer, that he'd recommended a plainer diet for her gorged favourite—such as mutton or beef—and a change of air to the seaside, with warm salt-water baths! The old lady actually allowed the plausible rascal a sum of money to take the dog to Scarborough and give it sea-baths and mutton broth (as *she* thought). Well! Padmore took the money, went to Scarborough with the dog, ate the mutton himself, and fed the dog on nothing but dry biscuits, and raced it religiously along at its utmost speed, with a string attached to its neck, for two hours every day. Of course, in a fortnight the dog was perfectly well, and the old lady was so delighted at the wonderful recovery of her favourite, that she appointed Padmore her own 'dog-doctor' for life, and the three repulsive-looking animals I saw with him were undergoing a course of treatment and sea-bathing (according to Padmore's bulletins to the old lady), to reduce their bulk and give them appetites to gorge themselves afresh."

" Ha ! ha ! ha ! " laughed Dick. " That is capital. What a clever scoundrel ! And what a silly old lady she must have been to believe in him like that ! "

" Wait a bit ; you haven't heard the best part of the story yet. Padmore was over two years with the old lady, attending to her lap-dogs and generally bamboozling her, and he thought he had become a prime favourite, expecting to find himself handsomely remembered in her will when the old lady left this world for a better. Well, she did die in the course of the following year. And what do you think she left him ? The will set forth that she was in great anxiety about leaving her pet dogs behind ; but, as he had loved them so much always, she bequeathed all her Blenheim spaniels to her faithful servant, James Ebenezer Padmore ! The old lady had enjoyed a

handsome annuity in her lifetime, but had
nothing to leave behind at her death. Well,
Padmore was very savage at having been
so 'sold,' and his 'pals' chaffed him most
unmercifully about his fondness for old
ladies' lap-dogs. He got rid of the whole
tribe, and started once more on the turf—
this time as a jockey—but he was suspected
of foul riding at Newmarket, and suspended
from riding for two years. Then he became
a hansom cab-driver in London, and the last
I heard of him was that he had gone out
to Vienna as private trainer to Prince
Schwartzstein, and I suppose he must have
lost that place, and then wandered here
somehow."

"Rather a chequered career," remarked
Dick. "But here we are at Roseneck, and
there is the Beau Rivage."

Mr. Padmore never called on Dick or
Allison at the Beau Rivage; but in September, when they were at the races at
Baden-Baden, who should emerge from the
saddling paddock before the great race,

smiling and self-possessed, but that enterprising individual, mounted on the favourite
" Troubadour," and he subsequently won
in a walk " hands down."

Dick's twenty-first birthday was passed at
Baden-Baden, in October, but the " coming
of age " (so far as the festivities consequent
on that important event were concerned)
was to take place immediately on his
return home.

About the beginning of November, in
Brussels, Dick, feeling tired of travelling
about, determined to make a move homewards ; and accordingly they left Brussels
for Ostend, crossed over to Dover, and so
to London, staying there for one night.

The next day, to the delight of his
mother, he arrived at High Wynyard. She
met him at the hall door, embraced him
fondly, and, pushing the hair caressingly off
his forehead, said—

" My own darling boy, how changed you
are, and how handsome you have grown !
I can hardly kiss you for that moustache.

I have written all the invitations for the ball, and the people we must have staying at the house ; you will find all the answers in your own smoking-room. I hope I have asked the people you like, Dick. There is only one thing I want in this world now, and that is to see you with a nice wife, dear. Then I can settle down in the old dower-house, and become a foolish, doting old grandmamma. There's no one abroad, is there ? ''

"No, no, madre mia. Don't be alarmed. I have no wish to marry for a long time yet. But here's Allison, whom you have quite forgotten."

"Oh, how do you do, Mr. Allison ? I beg your pardon, I am sure. Will you come and have a cup of tea ? '' And Allison goes with Lady Nora into the drawing-room, whilst Dick walks into his study (scarcely an appropriate name for his "own" apartment), and looks over the pile of letters that lay on the table.

He turns them over rapidly, and throwing

the rest aside, selects three, opening the uppermost one, which ran as follows :—

"Bruce's College, Oxford, Thursday.

"DEAR RICHARD,

"My aunt Nora has been kind enough to invite me to stay at High Wynyard for the festivities consequent on your coming of age, and requested me to forward my reply to you.

"I am not much addicted to balls, as I generally have more serious occupations to pass my time with. Nevertheless, I shall do myself the pleasure of accepting Aunt Nora's kind invitation for next week.

"I trust that you have derived improvement, as well as enjoyment, from your continental tour, and

"Believe me, yours sincerely,

"REGINALD A. BURTON."

"Poor old Reggie! He seems more priggish than ever. How solemnly he writes for a cousin! But here is Sir Henry

Oldstead's handwriting. I wonder what *he* says. I hope he can come." And Dick opened and read the following letter :—

"Colchicum-on-Sea, Wednesday night.

" MY DEAR DICK,

"Your mother has written to tell me that you come of age next week, and to bid me to the dissipation which I suppose it entails. All these sort of things I regard as egregious tomfoolery; but, as it is to celebrate the birthday of my old friend's son, I cannot refuse you, my dear boy, and will drag my weary old body to High Wynyard next week.

"My sins,—and the gout,—have drawn me to this Babel of a watering-place. If there are ever any ' nice' people here, they had certainly left before my arrival, for the snobocracy is rampant at Colchicum-on-Sea. Its women are very loud in manner, and free and easy,—consequently rather objectionable. But how shall I describe the positive *awfulness* of the *jeunesse dorée* of that ilk? The males delight in raiment of exceeding striking patterns and most gaudy hue, and their manners are of the 'slap-bang, jolly-dog' style, which I so truly detest. They are most obnoxious to me, and I vow I never used to meet such people when I was younger. Where can they come from? What suburb shelters them, I wonder, when they are not inflicting themselves on the different English watering-places?

"Pity the sorrows of a poor old man (of an old grumbler, perhaps you will say), but this gout drives me nearly frantic, leaving me scarcely strength to subscribe myself,

"Yours always, most affectionately,
"HENRY OLDSTEAD."

"What an amusing letter!" said Dick, after perusing the above. "Just like him. The very fiercest exterior scarcely conceal-ing one of the kindest hearts that ever beat. What's this great sprawling name on the envelope of this letter? Oh—Loutish, is it?

I wonder what *he* says." And he tears open the envelope. It ran :—

"Loutish Castle, Thursday.

" MY DEAR WYNYARD,

"Your mother has written to say your coming of age is to be held next week, and I suppose, as a relation, I am expected to come.

"Mind you have a fire lighted in my room some days before; and I hope the claret will be better than the last time I was at High Wynyard, when your butler managed to shake it up like medicine.

"Yours in haste,

"LOUTISH."

"Humph! rather ungracious I call that. He's pretty cool, I must say. Well, never mind. By Jove! I must leave the rest of the letters for another time; there's hardly time to dress for dinner!" exclaimed Dick, glancing at the clock. And he rushes upstairs, just finishing a hasty toilette as the bell clangs from the tower.

It is a merry little party at dinner that evening at High Wynyard. Lady Nora is delighted to have her darling boy back again. Mr. Preston, the old clergyman, is also pleased to see Dick, whom he loves as his own son, and highly diverted by the conversation of Allison, who makes himself most agreeable; whilst Dick—well, Dick is thinking how heartily glad he is to be back again at his old home, after all his wanderings.

CHAPTER XVI.

THE COMING OF AGE.

" You must wake and call me early, call me early, mother
    dear ;
  To-morrow'll be the happiest time of all the glad new
    year."

TENNYSON.

THE day of the festivities dawns brilliantly, with a soft westerly wind, and sun warm enough to make even Sir Henry Oldstead admit that there were sometimes such autumn days in England as one might pine for in vain elsewhere.

Amongst the party staying in the house are comprised, first—*place aux dames*—the Countess of Lackrent, her handsome, imperious daughter, Lady Julia Heriot, and meek husband, who scarcely ever opened his mouth but to agree with his strong-minded spouse; and Sir Henry Oldstead, who, affecting a most fierce and *farouche* exterior and cynical conversation, was in reality one of the kindest, most soft-hearted of men, and meekest of Benedicts. His eyes glanced daggers at any one who addressed him, his very moustache (severely waxed and pointed) bristled with indignation if he were only suspected of a kind act; whereas, in reality, he was perpetually striving to do some one a kindness in secret.

From the neighbourhood, Sir John Mangold—a pompous, fussy, kind-hearted old country gentleman—with his wife and two pretty, fair-haired daughters. Sir John is a mighty breeder of shorthorn cattle, and a very Rhadamanthus on the magisterial bench.

Then Lord Loutish, a young man who had succeeded a year before to his estates. Lord Loutish had been allowed by his parents to " drag himself up," instead of bringing him up themselves as befitted his position. He had been left when a boy to the care of servants, and had almost lived in the stables; the consequence being that, whilst he was overbearing, selfish, and purse-proud, his conversation was generally freely seasoned with oaths and stable jargon. His father had been a cousin to Lady Nora; thus he claimed connection with the Wynyard family.

Our old friend Reginald Burton is here too, even stiffer and more priggish than when we saw him at Eton. Even before he speaks, you could read it in the stiffness of his stand-up collars, in the immaculate folds of his cravat, primly tied into a severely square bow.

Then there is Cecil Darnley, a light-hearted, if somewhat impecunious, life-guardsman from Windsor. He is cheery and debonair, as if he possessed Lord Loutish's rent-roll, and did not owe a six-pence; whereas his nominal income was but £600 a year, and, like the young man we wot of, he "will lay a thousand to ten" with the utmost sang-froid.

The rest of the party consisted of Mr. Wurzel, his wife, daughter, and first-born son, William, whose ideas seldom soar further than the outside turnip-field on his father's estate ; Mrs. Vardon, a gay young widow from London ; and Mr. Maule, also from the modern Babylon.

The tenants' dinner was held in a large tent in the park. The visitors had gone in whilst Dick made his speech to thank the farmers for drinking his health. Mr. Job Swede, as the oldest tenant, had proposed the toast of their landlord, and Dick had responded in the orthodox fashion, averring that it gave him great pleasure to see them all there, and expressed a hope of often seeing them there again. Whereupon, of course, great applause, and three cheers for " t' young squire."

" And a little un in for the ladies," Mr. Rooter had suggested to the chairman.

" And a little un in for the ladies, in course," gravely said Mr. Job Swede.

Then " the little un in " was duly given,

and, so far as the house party were concerned, the tenants' dinner was over. But
the farmers kept it up right royally, and at
nine o'clock began country dances, which
lasted until the small hours of the morning;
Dick, to the delight of that good lady,
opening the ball with Mrs. Swede in a
roystering "hands across and down the
middle," retiring then with the rest of the
house party.

Dick, as in duty bound, took old Lady
Lackrent into dinner that evening; but
Lady Julia Heriot sat on his left hand, and
the old lady (a determined old matchmaker)
was not the least displeased that he devoted
most of his attention to her daughter,
leaving her to enjoy in peace the delicate
entrées of M. Ortolan, the French cook.

Lady Julia is a strikingly handsome bru-
nette of an imperial style of beauty. She is
very tall, and the figure is slight, but faultless. The beauty of the face, however, is
marred by a haughty expression, and there
is none of that softness and look of

sympathy which ought to beam on every woman's countenance. Moreover, she gave her opinions very boldly and decidedly. Indeed, Lady Lackrent had said to her, on overhearing a conversation between her daughter and young Lord Bullion, when the young lady had been scornfully sarcastic to that unlucky youth, " My dear, you will never be a favourite with men if you go on in that way. You don't know the vanity of men. as I do. They are as weak as possible. Only show deference to their opinions, and forbear to argue with them, and they will most likely say of you, ' Very well-informed girl that. Sensible and quiet, too.' Men don't like women to be like themselves, my love. I am sure some of them would like to have a creature that couldn't say Bo! to a goose—who would meekly ask to be allowed the honour of mending her husband's stockings."

Lady Julia, glancing sideways now at Dick, wonders how any one can be so good-looking, and yet seem so perfectly unaware of the fact.

That youth, conscious of but entirely un-abashed by the calm scrutiny, turns and says, with a smile—

"Lady Julia, I have just been saying to your mamma that I meant to ask you to open the ball with me to-night. We are going to dance in the picture-gallery."

"Oh yes, Mr. Wynyard; I shall be very pleased, I am sure. Such a fine old room that picture-gallery is. And what a lovely floor for dancing!"

"I have got the Guards band down, and I hope we shall have a good ball," said Dick.

"Oh! that was very thoughtful of you. Their dance music is so delightful."

"Ah, you should hear Strauss's band at Vienna," said Dick. But at this moment Lady Nora looks warningly at Lady Lack-rent, and the ladies rise and sail out of the room; Dick diving under the table to rescue a fan, a handkerchief, and a pair of gloves, all the property of Lady Julia, and for the recovery of which that young lady rewards

him with a smile which fairly astonishes
her mother, who intercepts it, by its sweet-
ness.

Who knows what visions that smile may
not have conjured up in the veteran matchmaker's mind?   Mr. Wynyard was young
and good-looking.   High Wynyard was a
fine old place, and the property could not
be worth less than £12,000 a year, she
thought.   And Lady Lackrent is very attentive to her hostess in the drawing-room
after dinner, praising that lady's handsome
son, and admiring the quaint tapestry which
covered the walls of the ante-room.

About half-past nine the guests begin to
arrive, and the old people flock together in
the long drawing-room—the younger, as
soon as they can, into the picture-gallery,
where the —— Guards band begins to play
soon after ten o'clock.

Dick claims Lady Julia Heriot for a valse.
It is the lovely "Isar lieder;" and as the
two float gracefully down the room, Dick
feels that his Florence training stands him

in good stead, and finds time to compliment
his partner on her performance. Many a
head is turned as they move smoothly along
the polished oak floor, and, half involuntarily, many couples stop dancing to look at
them.

Lady Julia, almost reclining in Dick's
arms as they glide along, with her stately
head bent over his shoulder, whispers—

"Oh, don't stop, *please*, Mr. Wynyard; I
could go on for ever, I believe. Your
trois temps is just right, and our steps suit
so well."

At last the valse comes to an end, and
they stop just opposite the portrait of
Dorothy Wynyard.

"What a beautiful face that is!" exclaimed Lady Julia. "Which of your ances-
tresses is that, Mr. Wynyard?"

"Oh, that's Dorothy Wynyard. Sir Giles
killed her baby, you know, and she went
mad," replied Dick, rather awkwardly.

"Indeed! Yes, I remember the story
now," she returned, coldly. "But what a

good portrait that is of your mother, over the door. And there is mamma looking at us from the other side of the room. Take me back to her, please."

"What a handsome couple they make!" Lady Lackrent was saying to her hostess, peering at the pair through her double gold eyeglass. "Adolphus!" she continued, turning, and sharply tapping her husband on the shoulder with the eyeglass. "Why, I do believe you are asleep already!"

"No, not in the least, my love," replied that meek, henpecked peer. "What is it?"

"Mind you don't forget to ask Mr. Wynyard to come and shoot at Appleby next week."

"But, my love—— "

"Now, do be quiet, Adolphus, and do as I tell you for once. You had better go and take Lady Nora in to supper. They are going to have it in the banqueting-hall." And the obedient husband accordingly shuffled off slowly in search of his hostess, but (having mistaken his commander's orders) with the laudable intention of asking Lady Nora to dance, instead of offering her his somewhat feeble arm to conduct her to the old banqueting-hall.

Dick dances several more valses with Lady Julia in the course of the evening, and appreciates each as much as the first one. When the men are smoking their cigars after the ball, Lord Loutish taps Dick familiarly on the shoulder, and says, "I say, Wynyard, I'd advise you to look out, my boy. That girl means to catch you. She is a very good-looking one, and no mistake—high stepper, and shows breed, too—but, by Gad! I shouldn't like to run in double harness with her myself. If anything happened to upset her temper—whew! just look out for squalls, that's all. She'd never stop until she kicked herself clear of everything. No, no; give me that little light-coloured Mangold filly for choice. Not such showy action, you know, but light mouth, good temper and manners. Much quieter than the other. Better stayer, too, bet you a pony!"

"Well, I don't know," said Dick, rather stiffly. "Those quiet ones are the worst sometimes. 'Still waters run deep,' you know. But I don't want to marry anybody, Loutish, thank you. Good night, and pleasant dreams to you."

"All right, my boy; 'a nod is as good as a wink to a blind horse,' you know. Good night."

Dick, as he winds up his watch before going to bed, says, "I don't believe I paid more attention to Lady Julia to-night than to any other girl. What a coarse, brutal fellow Loutish is! Well, it was a capital ball, I must say, and I'm very sleepy."

So speaking, he jumps into bed, puts out the light, and in less than five minutes is sleeping the sleep of the just.

CHAPTER XVII.

THE GIPSY'S PROPHECY.

> "A gloom
> In her dark eye prophetic of the doom
> Heaven gives its favourites—early death."
> BYRON.

BREAKFAST at High Wynyard the morning after the ball is very late; nevertheless, but few put in an appearance, and most of the ladies partake of that repast in their own rooms.

Dick is seated at the head of his own table, however, rosy-looking and fresh, as if he had not been smoking up to nearly five that morning, and glancing over the correspondence which lies beside his plate. "Hullo! what's this, I wonder?" he exclaims, taking up an envelope which bears no post-mark, and has a card lying on the top, inscribed—

```
Mr. Hiram P. Moller,
                    Chicago, U.S.A.
```

The card conveys no sort of impression to his mind, so he tears open the envelope, and reads the letter inside, which ran as follows :—

"San Francisco, 3rd October.

" MY DEAR DICK,

" This will serve as a letter of introduction for Mr. Hiram Moller, the nephew of my senior partner, to whom I was mainly indebted for my start in life. Ask Hiram down to the old place, and be civil to him. You will find him, if a little rough, very shrewd and entertaining, and he is a first-rate shot—with a rifle almost invincible.

" I do not send any messages, for I am writing to your mother by the next mail; so wind up, hoping that you are very well, and will be able to pay some attention to Moller, for the sake of

"Your affectionate uncle,

"THOMAS LOUGHTON WYNYARD."

Dick gets up, rings the bell, and says to the footman who answers it, "How did this letter and card get here? Do you know, James?"

"Yessir. Jebb's boy brought them up first thing this morning. Gentleman staying at the Wynyard Arms, sir."

"Order the mail-phaeton to come round in half an hour. And, James! tell them to put in two horses of that new team of chestnuts I bought on Monday—the leaders, you had better say." And Dick hastily finishes his breakfast in a manner highly suggestive of indigestion to any one not blessed with the swallowing capabilities of an ostrich—which wily bird is popularly supposed to habitually dine off stone ginger-beer bottles and brass-headed nails, finishing up with a light chasse in the shape of a telegraph wire. Then he rushes up to his mother's room with Uncle Tom's letter in his hand.

He comes down the oak staircase a quarter of an hour later, lights a huge cigar in the hall, and joins a group on the steps, who are admiring the dark chestnuts in his mail-phaeton. They are, indeed, a handsome pair. Not a spot of white anywhere but a star on each forehead. They step wonderfully, and as Dick drives rapidly away down the avenue, Lord Loutish, knocking the ashes out of his pipe, remarks, with a jarring laugh, " Gad! they won't want a steam-roller to stamp down the stones in the roads about these parts; Wynyard's chestnuts will do that for them."

" I confess I think them a very handsome pair," says Sir Henry Oldstead, fiercely twisting his moustache, and glaring at the speaker.

" I only trust Richard did not give the dealer much more than their value," breaks in Burton; " he *is* so extravagant and thoughtless."

Sir Henry Oldstead growls inaudibly, and, turning on his heel, walks off towards the stables.

Meanwhile the chestnuts have made good progress, and Dick soon pulls up before the little village inn, and asks the smiling, obsequious Boniface for Mr. Moller.

"Yes, Master Dick—beg pardon, Mr. Wynyard. This way, sir, please;" and he opens a door, when they are half blinded by a volume of smoke which fills the room. As the clouds of tobacco clear away a little, they discover a small, spare, cadaverous-looking man reclining in an easy attitude in an armchair, with his feet upon the window-sill, and puffing industriously at a long churchwarden pipe. He rises on Dick's entrance, however, but without abandoning his pipe, and slowly puts out his hand, which is warmly grasped by that youth, who says, "Mr. Moller, I believe? I am so sorry only to have got your card and the letter this morning. We had a ball at High Wynyard last night which you might have enjoyed."

"Thank you kindly, sir, but I only arrived at the depôt by the late train. Then, as for the ball, I'm not very spry at hopping myself, though I don't object to see others twirling about."

"I hope you will come up to the house with me now, Mr. Moller. I have a phaeton waiting at the door, and I'll send a cart for your luggage when we get home. There is a large party staying in the house who may amuse you."

"You do me proud. I should like to see your mansion, sir," said Mr. Moller, slowly. "Mr. Wynyard out in America has often told me about his old home."

And so they drive off together, Mr. Moller looking at the chestnuts with the eye of a connoisseur in horseflesh, and admiring the giant oaks as they drive up the avenue.

Lady Nora receives the American with her usual quiet courtesy, and Mr. Moller, seated next to his hostess at luncheon, waxes most loquacious, and strives to initiate that

somewhat bewildered lady in the mysteries
of cunning Yankee drinks, such as " corpse
revivers," " gin sling," and " brandy cock-
tails "—all of which, he gravely assures his
astonished châtelaine, will make her hair
curl with pleasure."

After luncheon Dick says, " Let us make
up a riding party, and go over to see the old
abbey. Mr. Moller, do you ride ? Lady
Julia,—Miss Mangold,—will you go ? Miss
Wurzel, I have a cob called Syntax, steady
as a rock, which will just suit you. Mrs.
Vardon, you could ride the roan mare
Syringa, and there are hacks enough for
all the men. Loutish, you can ride that
black mare, Reine Margot, if you like. I
am told she is a perfect devil; but you like a
little horsebreaking, and don't care about
having an easy mount, I know."

"I have brought you a grey mare as a
present, Dick," interrupted Sir Henry Oldstead. " Not quite up to your weight, I'm
afraid ; but she will make a perfect lady's
hack. Any one with hands could ride her.

You had better offer her to Lady Julia for this afternoon."

Finally, Lady Julia and the elder Miss Mangold decide to ride, Mrs. Vardon going as chaperone with them, and mounts were provided for Lord Loutish and the American; Dick choosing a bay mare called Belle Hélène for himself. Then Lady Lackrent went out in the barouche with her hostess, Sir Henry Oldstead and Mrs. Wurzel occupying the back seat; whilst Lord Lackrent and Sir John Mangold walked off to the home farm, the rest of the party engaging [in lawn-tennis on the bowling-green, under the care of Reginald Burton and Allison.

Lady Julia looked well on horseback, and was fully aware of the fact. The neat, tight-fitting, dark-blue habit showed off her almost faultless figure to advantage; and her hair was neatly drawn back off the forehead, and fastened in a simple knot behind, under a felt hat which suited her admirably.

She takes a little longer to mount than is

perhaps strictly necessary, Dick at length swinging her lightly into the saddle. As the grey mare gives a violent plunge, and begins bucking in a most uncomfortable manner, it is evident that Lady Julia wishes to rule more by fear than love, for she gives her two stinging cuts on the shoulder, which cause her to rear violently; and Lord Loutish, nudging Dick in the side, says, in a loud whisper, "Awkward, my boy, if she manages her husband at all like her horse."

The American mounts a steady brown cob called Captain, and Lord Loutish bestrides the refractory Reine Margot, of which Dick had given such a doubtful character. And she does her utmost to deserve it; first standing on her hind legs, then resolutely planting her fore feet in the gravel, refusing to move until admonished by a sharp dig of the spur, when she bounds forward with a jerk that nearly dislocates Lord Loutish's shoulder.

Lady Julia is highly pleased with the grey she sits so gracefully, and, after a long swinging canter, in which the mare holds her own gallantly over the soft elastic turf, she pats her on the shoulder, and, turning to Dick, says—

"I think this is a charming present from Sir Henry. I see you name all your horses, Mr. Wynyard. What shall you call this one?"

"Oh, I don't know. Primrose, Daisy, Buttercup, Daffodil—anything you like," returned Dick.

"Ah! you like flowers as names best, I see," said Lady Julia, softly. "Well, call her—— Let me see;" and she meditates for a few moments, and then says, suddenly and hurriedly, "Call her Rose d'Amour, Mr. Wynyard."

"Rose——" begins Dick; but his companion, touching her mare sharply with the whip, joins the American and Mrs. Vardon, who are riding in front.

They admire the ruins of the abbey, and as they are returning home in the November twilight, Dick's mare suddenly starts violently, nearly unseating her rider, and swerves across the road close to the ditch at the side.

"So-ho! steady, old gal," said Dick, patting his mare. "What is it, my Belle Hélène?"

At this moment an old woman, in a long grey cloak and old-fashioned bonnet, comes out of the shadow and looks fixedly at the party.

"What, old Mother Bell, is that you?" exclaims Dick. "How are you? I haven't seen you for years!"

"I'm middling, thank you, Master Dick; and how's yourself? And who's the bonnie dark lady beside you?" said the old woman, fixing her keen bright eyes on Lady Julia's face. "Shall I be telling any of your fortunes, gentlefolks, to-day? Give me your own hand first, Master Dick." And Dick, throwing a sovereign carelessly to her, places his long slim member in the old woman's horny, wrinkled palm.

"Eh! but there's many a line in your

palm, my bonnie boy. All these small lines mean many a journey in foreign parts; but never a long one. Whether past or to be I know not. Then this large one—— Ha! what's this?" exclaimed the old dame, peering closer. "Here's the cruel sea, and a long, long journey over it, and a weary while away. Then that cross line means sorrow a-coming home to you, my lad; and that crooked mark is a woman in it, and her ways are crooked like that line. Ride on, my bonnie boy, ride on, with your bright youth and your handsome face; but you cannot ride away from the sorrow that must surely come to you, if Mother Bell knows aught about it."

"What bosh, Wynyard!" exclaimed Lord Loutish. "Just as if a fellow with a property to look after would be likely 'to see the cruel sea, and a long, long journey over it,'" said he, mimicking the old woman's voice.

She turned on him angrily, and said, "How now, my scoffing cuckoo? I'll tell

you something about yourself that will stop
your jeering. I know you, my Lord of
Loutish; and mark my words"—and she
shook her finger threateningly at him—"by
coal you have your living, and by coal shall
you have your death, and then—all to dust.
Beware!"

Lord Loutish affected to laugh, but it
died away on his lips. He derived most
of his income from coal mines, and some
years after this adventure he went down
into one of them with his manager. Suddenly there was a loud explosion in the
mine, and the bodies of Lord Loutish and
his factotum were brought up the following
day, horribly mangled and hardly recogniz-
able. So the old gipsy's prophecy was fear-
fully fulfilled to the letter in his case.

The American now turns to Mother Bell,
and says politely, "May I ask you, ma'am,
if you are the seventh daughter of a seventh
son? Ah! that's real curious. I thought
you would be, somehow."

"I can tell you about yourself, foreigner

though you be," began the old woman; but
Miss Mangold, almost sobbing with terror,
says, " Oh, *please* let us ride on, Mr. Wynyard; I *am* so frightened!"

" Certainly, Miss Mangold. I am very
sorry I spoke to her at all, now. Good
night, mother," he calls out gaily. "You
have given us all the horrors with your
fortune-telling."

Dick thinks his companion strangely
silent, as they ride back to High Wynyard;
and Lady Julia outwardly wonders "how
Mr. Wynyard and Mr. Moller can go on
joking after hearing such dreadful things"
—in her heart secretly admiring them both
for their indifference to the old crone's
prophecies.

CHAPTER XVIII.

IN THE SMOKING-ROOM.

> "Sublime tobacco! which from east to west
> Cheers the tar's labour, or the Turcoman's rest;
> Which on the Moslem's ottoman divides
> His hours, and rivals opium and his brides."
>
> BYRON.

THE ladies had retired—ostensibly, to their own apartments; in reality (with the exception of the elder ones), to talk over the men of the party, in the Miss Mangolds' room.

Ye Gods! how our ears would tingle sometimes, could we overhear the conversations of the "Hair-brush Club!" Loose dressing-gowns and slippers, when the back-hair is let down, seem to conduce to confidence with the female sex in the same way

as the male "last" cigar. Talk of five-
o'clock tea, indeed, of which it has been
said, "With every sip a reputation dies!"
— the Hair-brush Club could, in sporting
parlance, give more than a stone and a
beating. For every tale that the cups, into
which the invigorating bohea is poured,
could tell, the dressing-gowns and hair-
brushes could repeat a dozen. How many
a marriage has been prevented, I wonder,
by the disparaging remarks made at these
feminine nocturnal gatherings at country
houses? Phyllis may have a secret pen-
chant for Corydon, but when she hears the
abuse showered on his devoted head by her
"dear friends," it may vanish like snow
under the fierce fire of their raillery. And
how can Chloe still admire Strephon, when
she hears him dubbed awkward, red-haired,
and stupid, by the female chorus of detractors? Would fair, false Helen of Troy
have eloped with Paris, if she had met him
at a country house, and heard that fascinating youth talked over at one of these

nocturnal gatherings? And how much love would Venus have borne for Adonis, if she had had fair confidantes to call him a milksop and a conceited muff, instead of trusting to her own wilful judgment and wild passion alone? What chance would Antony have had, if Cleopatra and Octavia could have talked him over whilst combing out their dusky locks? Do you think that the doubtless excellent moral qualities of pious Æneas would have proved so destructive to Dido's peace of mind, if that fond, foolish queen had allowed her hand-maidens to pronounce him a tiresome bore in her presence?

When the last dress had vanished up the oak staircase, Dick said, " Now, then, who's for a cigar? Burton, I know you don't smoke. Loutish, will you have one?"

" No, thanks; I am rather out of sorts, and shall go to bed early to-night. I don't want anything. I've got some brandy in my own bedroom," he added, with a cunning leer.

"What a cub that boy is!" exclaimed Sir Henry Oldstead, when the smoking-room door is shut. "The brandy bottle is his 'fidus Achates.' He is always at it."

"Well, sir," said the American, "if that is a specimen of your hereditary legislator, I don't cotton to the institution. We don't raise our rulers in the States like that, sir. We are a young country, and likely many of us are a bit uncertain about our grand-fathers; but we couldn't stomach a man who was a monstrous fool to legislate for us, only because his father or grandfather was a peer of the realm, and had done so before him. No, sir! To a free-born American the institution of hereditary legislation seems rotten — rotten to the core, I say, sir!" he continued, excitedly, striking his hand on the table, and making the bottles and glasses on it ring again.

"But, my dear Mr. Moller," said Mr. Wurzel, blandly, "you mistake. Young Loutish has no voice in the government of the country, fortunately; and, what is more—— "

"Don't tell me that, sir," interrupted the American, impetuously. "Can't he go down to your house of legislation when there is some useful bill, maybe, to be passed, and vote against it, with as many idiots like himself who may be found available at the last moment, sir? I say, can't he—— "

"Do try one of these regalias, Mr. Moller, won't you?" interposed Dick. "They are some that Uncle Tom got for me, and you know what a judge of tobacco he is."

"He is that, sir," said the American, soothed by the fragrant fumes of his favourite plant. "I call this a downright good weed. Have you many of them, sir?"

"What a good joke it is," said Allison, *sotto voce*, to Cecil Darnley, "that Moller should abuse our institutions so fiercely, when Americans are even more snobbish and lord-idolatrous than vulgar English people! If by chance they come across a peer abroad, don't they just kotow to him, and milord him. Hang all republics, I say. What is a president, I should like to know, but a sort of king?"

"Very true, very true," sleepily assented Darnley.

"Now then, Cis, wake up," said Dick. "How you were snoring just now!"

"Talking about snoring, sir," said the American, turning his chair round, "I remember a story of a man down Newhaven way, in Connecticut, who snored most dreadful loud, he did, and disturbed his neighbours frightful. At last he got so tarnation bad, that he was obliged actually to sleep in the next room, for fear of disturbing even himself."

Roars of laughter greeted this sally, and Allison said, "Apropos of American stories, Mr. Moller, I remember one. I think it was Mark Twain's, but I'm not sure; anyhow, it was one of your countrymen who told it. It seems that earthquakes are very frequent in the South American republics; and an anxious father, apprehending one in his city, sent his boys, who were home from school for the holidays, away to a friend, until the earthquake should have passed over. Three days after they had gone, he received a letter from his friend, saying, 'Dear ——, Send the earthquake down here, if you like; but for Heaven's sake take your boys away!'"

"Smart, sir, very smart," allowed Mr. Moller, coolly, not moving a muscle of his face. But the rest went off into peals of laughter; Mr. Wurzel almost choking himself into a fit at Allison's dry manner in relating the story.

"You were abusing our institutions just now, Mr. Moller," said Mr. Wurzel, when he had recovered himself a little; "and no doubt you think that our English law courts want reform, with the rest; but what do you say to this? I read the other day, in a French newspaper, that a man had been very properly found guilty of having murdered both his father and mother, but the jury recommended the prisoner to mercy. 'On what grounds?' asked the judge. 'Oh, there are extenuating circumstances. He is an orphan,' replied the foreman of the jury. Now, pray, what do you think of that, eh?"

All laughed, and Darnley said, "Talking of France and French newspapers, I remember I was over in Paris at the time that Sir Bartle Frere was sent out to Zanzibar, to suppress the slave trade, which was pretty actively carried on in Sejd Burghash's territory. Well, one morning I bought a French newspaper at a kiosque on the Boulevards— I won't say which one it was—and, in glancing over the 'general intelligence' column, I was gratified to learn that the English were a very enterprising nation; because, although Baker Pasha had only just returned from trying to suppress the slave trade, 'the Sir Bartle frères' had been sent out with the same laudable object. Not bad that, was it? How

Sanderson and I did laugh over the Frenchman's mistake, to be sure!"

"Oh, by the way, where is Tom Sanderson now?" asked Wynyard. "I want to ask him to come and shoot here."

"Then you'll have to send out the invitation to Allahabad. Tom Sanderson was awfully hard hit over last Doncaster meeting, and he exchanged into the —th, who had just gone out to India."

"A very good thing too. There's one infernal fool the less in England, in that case," remarked Sir Henry Oldstead, contemptuously. "I never could abide that stupid young man."

"Oh, come—come now, Sir Henry," said Wynyard, deprecatingly, "he wasn't such a bad fellow. I never heard him say an ill-natured thing of any one in his life."

"How could he possibly talk ill of anybody, my dear boy, when he never, by any chance, spoke of any one but his own idiotic self?" rejoined Sir Henry, triumphantly.

"Perhaps you like his brother 'the

Buffer,' who used to be in my regiment, better?" asked Darnley.

"'Arcades ambo!' Infernal young fools both," replied Sir Henry, irascibly. "They are about on a par, as to intelligence, with that young cub Loutish, who would probably lose his situation if he were a groom in the stables—the only place his manners and intelligence entitle him to," he added, fiercely twisting the ends of his carefully waxed moustache.

"Try another of these Partagas, Sir Henry; they are from Carlin, and the same you always smoke yourself. You like them full-flavoured, I know," said Wynyard.

" May I trouble you, too, sir?" said the American, putting his hand into the box and selecting four with great care. "Prime tobacco, Mr. Wynyard, sir, prime. Regular eye-openers, I call these weeds, sir. That was a queer rigmarole of the old lady's this afternoon, warn't it? Curious—I never knew a fortune-teller yet who wasn't the seventh daughter of a seventh son, sir," he added, sarcastically, emitting a volume of smoke from his lips, as if puffing away the superstition.

"Wonderful old woman, Sally Bell," said Dick. "Believe she is over a hundred. She gave it to Loutish pretty hot for laughing at her."

"Is that old Sally Bell of Cuddington you are talking of? Why, I have known her these forty years," said Mr. Wurzel; "I think she really must be over a hundred. The villagers all swear she is a hundred and twenty-four!"

"Oh! I say, draw it mild, Mr. Wurzel," broke in Darnley, somewhat incredulously.

"Fact, I assure you, Mr. Darnley," returned Mr. Wurzel, pompously. "I remember her quite well predicting to old Godfrey Wynyard that his eldest son should never die in his bed, but that he would meet his death by a gun. That was your poor father," he continued, turning to Dick, "and old Godfrey Wynyard never would let him shoot as a boy. I recollect how

angry your poor father used to be when
your uncle Tom and aunt Margaret used
to tease him about being coddled, and not
allowed to carry a gun, when the coverts
were shot here. But all the precautions
could not save him, poor fellow. Sally Bell
was right. I can't say that she anticipated
the Russian bullet, but she certainly pre-
dicted he would meet his death by a
gun."

"Well, that certainly was very curious,"
admitted Sir Henry. "Àpropos of prophecies, in Northshire we swear by Mother
Shipton. Her prophecies were really extraordinary; and most of them have been
verified, too. She was born, I believe, about
1480, in the reign of Henry VII. I remember, in a field near Eborton, there used to
be a stone figure of her, in a tall, steeple-
crowned hat; and the prophecy used to
frighten me when a boy tremendously."

"Oh, do give it to us," exclaimed Allison;
"I am always interested in these old legends
and prophecies."

"Well, I am half afraid I may have forgotten it now," said Sir Henry, "but I will try to remember it as I go along;" and, putting down his cigar, he bégan

"MOTHER SHIPTON'S PROPHECY.

"Carriages without horses shall go,
And accidents fill the world with woe.
Around the world thoughts shall fly
In the twinkling of an eye.
Water shall yet more wonders do ;
Now strange—but yet they shall be true.
The world upside down shall be,
And gold be found at the root of a tree.
Through hills man shall ride,
And no horse or ass be at his side.
Under water man shall walk,
Shall ride, shall sleep, shall talk.
In the air men shall be seen,
In white, and black, and green.
Iron in the water shall float
As easy as a wooden boat.
Gold shall be found, and shown
In land that is not now known.
Fire and water shall wonders do.
England shall at last admit a Jew.
The world to an end shall come
In eighteen hundred and eighty-one."

"By Jove !" exclaimed Wynyard. "That is an extraordinary prophecy. Why, every

single thing has come true, except the last
two lines."

"Yes," observed Allison, sarcastically.
"Rather a bore, though, for people who
have taken long leases of their houses."

"By Jingo!" exclaimed Darnley. "Don't
talk of such a thing, Allison. I'm not half
tired of life yet. You quite give one the
horrors. Let's go and 'draw' that sancti-
monious prig Burton to shake the blue
devils off us—eh, Dick?"

"No, no!" returned that youth, good-
naturedly. "Poor Reggie! he would be in
such a rage. There mustn't be any bear-
fighting in my house, Cis. Besides, we
might disturb my mother. I think we had
better have a rubber, or else a game of
billiards."

And so all adjourn to the billiard-room,
which opens out of the smoking-room.
Dick is skilful with a cue, and Allison
is a brilliant player, but no one can cope
with the wily American at pool. He
pockets his adversaries' balls with the

utmost ease, picking up the five-shilling "lives" with unconcealed satisfaction; and then, with affected nonchalance, places his own ball safe under the cushion behind another, whence it is impossible to take a "life" off him; by these skilful tactics securing three pools in succession, and about seventeen sovereigns. It was really extraordinary the strokes he made. Mr. Moller did not appear to play so brilliantly, but the instant any one offered to *bet* against his stroke, it was extraordinary to witness the ease with which he accomplished it, and the chuckle with which he pocketed the wager.

CHAPTER XIX.

AN OLD ACQUAINTANCE REAPPEARS.

"To buy his favour I extend this friendship : '
If he will take it, so ; if not, adieu !
And for my love, I pray you wrong me not."

SHAKESPEARE.

ON Sunday most of the party walked to church. Indeed, it was in the park, only a few hundred yards distant from the house —one of those curious old parish churches, of which, alas ! so few remain now.

A curate of High Church proclivities had once suggested that the old square, high-backed pews should be removed, and those abominable, cramped, open sittings (where your neighbours behind can wind up their watches in your ear, or look cruelly at the fast-thinning hair on the top of your head)

substituted for them. He was regarded
with open-mouthed horror at the vestry
meeting when he broached his proposal,
and was ever after looked upon as a Goth
by his conservative parishioners. Indeed,
it was whispered (but even his bitterest
detractors refused to quite believe such a
wild assertion) that the curate actually
wished to have a choir robed in white
surplices, and an organ—not to speak of
a professional organist—in place of the
harmonium played by the village school-
mistress.

"Whoy, the man must be clean daft,"
had said that great oracle, Farmer Job
Swede, at a vestry meeting, when some one
had mentioned (with bated breath) this
contemplated audacious reform.

Soon after, the curate left High Wynyard
for a London suburb, where he gave his
unfortunate parishioners two services every
week-day, and three on the Sabbath, and
Mr. Preston had never supplied his place
since.

The rector was of the good old-fashioned sort of parson, who thought, if he gave his congregation two services every Sunday, and visited them when they were sick, he had done his duty by them. He liked his bottle of port, did not think he sinned deeply if he walked with a gun when the Wynyard coverts were shot, and had been known to appear at the meet of the Gorse-top Hounds, on his fat old cob the Bishop. And then—O great and good man! as he was strong, so was he merciful—he timed himself in the length of his sermons; and never preached more than his quarter of an hour. On one occasion, indeed (a sermon for a subscription to send out white hats and frock-coats to the South Sea Islanders, a project he secretly thought little of), Mr. Preston was almost tedious. He often re-counted with a chuckle, that when he after-wards asked old Farmer Rooter, "Well, Graffar, and how did you like my sermon to-day?" that old worthy had shaken his white head sententiously, and observed gravely, "Eh, passon, but you was long ower yer proper toime, surelie."

Mr. Preston did not encourage visiting the cotters in the parish, except in the case of Lady Nora Wynyard. And, indeed, how much may not this be overdone when there are too many ladies in a parish? Do we not know of a village where, if rumour lies not, a certain lady visitor taking a (perfectly well-to-do) family a packet of tea, the gift was not accepted with grace or alacrity? "Oh, do have the tea," said the lady visitor, and added hurriedly in a whisper, "I'll give you a shilling if you will!"

The rector and parish of High Wynyard were conservative to the backbone, and so the old church had remained as it was. Dick and his party, going into the squire's pew, enter by a separate door from the churchyard, and go into a comfortable room with a blazing fire. There is a window on one side to be thrown up before they are in church at all, and on the other, an oriel

window of stained glass, bearing the Wynyard arms and other devices, looks out over
the park.   The effigy of stout old Sir Miles
de Wynyarde reclines at full length on a
tomb, side by side with Dame Hildegarde,
his wife, in the centre of the church, his
battered helmet being hung up with rows of
others above.   That doughty warrior, with
many an ancestor of Dick's, lies buried
underneath the flags of the middle aisle—
all, in fact, down to Sir Hugh Wynyard,
whose last resting-place on earth is in a
vault adjoining the church, and in which
his descendants had been subsequently in-
terred.

The worthy rector goes through the service at a respectable pace, and his sermon
is just under the usual quarter of an hour.
Dick afterwards stops in the churchyard to
shake hands with Mr. Preston and some of
the farmers; and the American, much to
that old lady's annoyance, gravely presents
his arm for Lady Lackrent's acceptance.
She affects not to see it; but Mr. Moller

is not to be denied, and politely bars her path. Finally, to the delight of Allison and Darnley, who laugh consumedly, the ill-assorted pair march off slowly, arm-in-arm.

"Pity, ma'am," says the American, with a wave of his unoccupied arm, "that the church is so old and mouldy. Give me a spick and span new edifice, say I, of red brick, or something smartish to look at."

Lady Lackrent slowly lifts her gold eye-glass, and says patronizingly, and as disdainfully as she dares—

"My dear Mr. Moller, you Americans are a new people, and can't understand the value of antiquities. *I* think that High Wynyard church is beautiful. I only wish ours at Appleby was as old;" and she drew herself up majestically.

"Bully for you, ma'am," rejoined the American, perfectly unmoved. "I don't think you're right; but you are a woman, and consequently right down impossible to argue with at all reasonable like."

"Sir!" exclaimed Lady Lackrent.

"No offence, ma'am—no offence," said Mr. Moller, affably. "We each stick to our own o-pinion. What a fat lady that party in church with the green gown and blue bonnet was, to be sure! Re-minds me, ma'am, of a friend of mine down New Orleans way, who had a wife that awful fat, that on Sundays he always declared he would like to make two journeys in his vehicle to fetch her back again from church, instead of taking her all at once."

"Adolphus!" gasped out Lady Lackrent, "come here directly!" But that peer, wise in his generation, conveniently turns his deaf ear to the frantic appeal of his strong-minded spouse.

"Snakes! Now, you're never going to feel riled, ma'am, are you?" asked the American, affecting concern. "Now, people show their anger in different ways," he continued, reflectively. "I did once hit a man in anger, ma'am, and there remained in his place nothing but a grease spot after the blow."

"Adolphus! *will* you come here!" almost screamed Lady Lackrent, stamping her foot. "Odious—vulgar—man that is!" she continued, almost breathless with passion, to her husband, when she got away.

"Now, my love, pray don't excite yourself unnecessarily. You know, Doctor——"

"Oh, you are too bad, Adolphus! You'd provoke a saint, I declare——" But here Lord Lackrent's previous experiences prompt him to shuffle on quickly, and he loses the rest of his partner's complaints.

"Got her dander up, the tarnation affected, stuck-up old cat," muttered the American to Allison. "Only wish I may see her out Chicago way. Wouldn't I just give her fits!"

Lady Lackrent's ruffled feathers are somewhat smoothed by an excellent luncheon and several glasses of dry sherry, and she expresses her intention to her hostess of going to church again in the afternoon.

"Sir Henry," said Dick, after luncheon, "I want you to come out and give me your

advice about some new stables. I am
thinking of making private training quarters
in the park, and want to begin racing on a
large scale. I have engaged a trainer
already, and bought a few horses. There
have always been a few brood mares here,
you know, and there are several good-looking yearlings and two-year-olds in the
paddocks."

"I shall be very pleased to give you my
advice, my dear boy. But do you think
you are quite wise in starting on the turf?
You know, Dick," he added, " your income,
though a very good one, is not unlimited;
yet you play very high, and keep up everything here, as if you had the magic purse of
Fortunatus at your command."

"Oh! I am better off than my grandfather was, because of my long minority;
and there is some ready money, besides
a deal of timber that might be thinned.
Light a cigar, Sir Henry, before you go out,
won't you?" And Dick selects a huge
Cabana for himself.

They walk out together, coming across Allison and Darnley on their way to the stables; and when they get to the stud-groom's cottage, to Allison's extreme astonishment, who should step out of it and salute him but Mr. James Padmore, smiling and stroking his bullet-head as of old.

"Why, Padmore, whatever are you doing here?" asked Allison.

"Well, you see, sir, Squire Wynyard has engaged me as private trainer for his 'orses. We're agoin' on the turf, Mr. Allison," replied Mr. Padmore, smiling approvingly. And then, turning round and touching his hat to the others, he said, "Good day, Sir 'Enery. Hopes I sees you well, sir?"

"Well, Padmore, how are you? I am glad to see you have got a place. We have come down to see the horses."

"Bring out Undine first, Padmore," said Dick.

"Yessir," replies that bustling, active individual, and in a few minutes they are introduced to a very handsome bay mare,

with black points.   The cloth is lightly
stripped off, and she is a picture to look at ;
but, irritated by the cold east wind blowing
on her quarters, lashes out viciously,
narrowly missing Mr. Padmore's bullet-
head.

"A little temper," remarks that unmoved
individual, coolly.   "Only the sex, Sir
'Enery.   They wants humourin', they does.
Dreadful uncertain like in their tempers,
they is."

"An uncommonly good-looking mare
when her coat gets a little better.   What is
she entered for, Dick?" asks Sir Henry;
"and how is she bred?"

"She's by Norseman, out of Mermaid.
Unfortunately not in for the Derby; but
she's entered for the cup at Ascot, and the
St. Leger at Doncaster, next year, amongst
her bigger engagements.   But I've eight
more in training here.   Let's go on and
look at them."

After these are paraded, they go and
inspect the yearlings and brood mares, Sir

Henry bestowing unqualified approval on his young friend's judgment in horseflesh.

"Whatever made you engage that fellow Padmore, Dick?" asked Allison, as they walked back to the house.

"Oh, I don't know. I found a letter from him from London when I got down here. I thought he was a shrewd, clever fellow, and so engaged him. I confess I was half ashamed to tell you of it, old fellow."

Mr. Padmore, after the inspection of his department is over, makes his subordinates bustle about in a manner that argues considerable practice. One luckless wight drops Undine's feed in carrying it across the yard, and Mr. Padmore, argus-eyed and stern, accosts the unfortunate delinquent with polished, cutting sarcasm, adjuring him "to put 'is stoopid 'ead in a nosebag," and inquires witheringly (with sundry oaths, and in different language) if he were only born yesterday; also, if his maternal relative ever intrusts him with eggs to take to

market. Finally, he bids the trembling Bob
Shaver approach the august presence, and
says, " Now then, young fellow, what d'yer
think 'ud have 'appened to me if I'd dropped
a 'orse's feed?   I was just in your place like
once."

" No, was you, though?" said Bob
Shaver, admiringly ; " and you've riz to be
what you are !" surveying, almost with awe,
the architect of such a fortune.

Mr. Padmore is mollified. After all, is
he not human?—and vanity is the besetting
sin of all. He strokes his well-shorn chin
complacently, and says blandly, " Well, run
along, young feller, now, and don't do it
again, that's all." Afterwards, he comes
to the conclusion that Bob Shaver is a
smartish lad after all.

Dick and his companions meet the rest
of the party returning from church through
the shrubbery, and, the day being fine, all
walk off to inspect the dairies and home
farm, where the younger ladies go into
ecstasies over a family of juvenile Berkshire

pigs, voting them "such dear little white
darlings, you know;" and Dick delights Sir
John Mangold by expressing his intention
of breeding shorthorns, and asking his
valuable opinion as to the respective merits
of a prize "Duchess" cow, and an obese
Hereford monster, which is fattening for the
slaughter-house.

Then they go on to the kennels, where
Mrs. Vardon takes an especial fancy to an
old retriever lady, with a large and thirsty
family clamouring around her; the Miss
Mangolds, with more practised country
eyes, admiring some fine Irish setters; and
Miss Wurzel begs to be presented with a
tiny Gordon setter pup. Dick smilingly
gives it to her at once, and Miss Wurzel
ties her pocket-handkerchief round its neck,
and marches the unfortunate little animal—
squealing loudly—away.

In Godfrey Wynyard's day, the Gorsetop
Hounds had had their kennels at High
Wynyard; and the party inspect the build-
ings, which seem to want considerable

repair. Lord Lackrent, as a leading sports-
man in the county, asks Dick whether he
would emulate his grandsire, and hunt the
Gorsetop Hounds, should the mastership of
that celebrated pack become vacant, as
anticipated, owing to the increasing years
of Mr. Winnbush.

Need we say that Dick eagerly assents,
in spite of Sir Henry's warnings, and in his
mind is already rebuilding the kennels for
the hounds, and divers other castles in the
air?

The following morning Lord Loutish took
his departure, having remained in bed all
Sunday; and the rest spent the day in
shooting part of the coverts, when the
American acquitted himself brilliantly,
knocking over the hares, and bringing down
the rocketers, with considerable *aplomb*.
The younger ladies, under the chaperonage
of gay Mrs. Vardon, come out with the
luncheon, and afterwards Lady Julia insists
on standing near Dick at the corner of a
ride, much to the discomposure of that

youth, who misses three cock pheasants in succession, eliciting a growl from the old head keeper to his subordinates of "What bizniss has ladies to be a-comin' with the guns, a-puttin of 'em horf like that, by talking to 'em on the shot?"

The next morning there was a hunt breakfast at High Wynyard, and hospitality was offered to all alike, irrespective of station or acquaintance. The Gorsetop Hounds trot off punctually at 11.30, at the heels of Will Scarlet the huntsman, to draw the coverts. It is a good scenting day, and soon a whimper is heard from one hound, quickly followed by a chorus of melody from the rest of the pack. Will Scarlet lifts his cap and screams out, "Go-o-orn away, gorn away—yo-icks—for-rard!" and, ramming the spurs into his horse's flanks, is soon over the fence and with the hounds, which are streaming across the park with the scent nearly breast high.

Dick is supposed to be piloting Lady Julia, but the instant the hounds break covert he forgets — to that young lady's chagrin—her existence, in the excitement. He gets a bad start, but catching his big black horse Pluto hard by the head, sends him at a stiff-looking gate. Lady Julia watches him involuntarily, and gives a sigh of relief as Pluto hits the top rail hard with his hind hoofs, but, recovering himself, gallops across a grass field at racing pace.

They have a clinking run, straight as a die, to Oulburn Shaws; and Dick, returning about five o'clock, happy, hungry, and splashed with mud from head to foot, informs the American, whom he meets at the gate, that the gallant fox had gone to earth at Oulburn Shaws about four, and was left to furnish a run for another day.

The next two days were employed in shooting some more outlying coverts, varied by a little partridge driving; and on Saturday the party broke up. The American, Allison, and Sir Henry Oldstead accept an invitation from hospitable old Sir John Mangold. Cecil Darnley goes back to barracks at Windsor; Burton to Bruce College, Oxford, intending to read for "honours;" Mrs. Vardon to London; and the Wurzels to Millett Hall. Dick, after accepting an invitation to shoot at Appleby the following week with Lord Lackrent, accompanies their carriage to the south lodge, and there bids them good-bye.

That evening, to Lady Nora's delight, she has a *tête-à-tête* dinner with her darling son, and is inexpressibly gratified afterwards, when he plays her favourite game of Bezique, showing an utter recklessness in marking his points, which enables her to defeat him five games in succession.

CHAPTER XX.

THE MEET OF THE COACHING CLUB.

"And pray, what can Tommy Onslow do?
  Why, he can drive a chaise and two.
  What! and can Tommy Onslow do no more?
  Yes! for he can drive a coach and four!"

A MILD, sunny morning in the beginning of May. The gummy horse-chestnut buds have all opened, and most of the trees in Kensington Gardens and the Park are nearly in full leaf. We see that the flower-beds are planted out, as we walk down from Grosvenor Gate towards Apsley House.

What a crowd there is by the Achilles statue, lining both sides of the road by the Serpentine as far as one can see, and we recollect that the Coaching Club meet at the Powder Magazine this morning.

Let us go up there and see the muster of the coaches. All along, on each side of the road, we notice hosts of faces that we know and see "everywhere," as we hear some one observe. (What a comprehensive term, by the way, is this "everywhere"!) Here is a royal princess, whose kindly face and cheery smile are always pleasant to behold; she rarely misses a meet of either the Four-in-hand or the Coaching Club, and her open carriage is generally filled, on these occasions, with her children. There is a noble ex-Master of the Buckhounds, bestriding a clever white hack and talking to a prominent member of the Opposition, who has the reputation of being able, amongst other accomplishments, to make the best bow in Europe. On the showy black is a figure we have missed of late years in London. How cruel of him to bewitch the Parisian world alone by his admirable horsemanship! But here comes the policeman on his white steed, clearing the road for the passage of an approaching drag. It belongs to the noble president of the club (the " Duke of Sport," as he has been aptly named by a clever weekly journal), and is driven by one of his sons, with the heir-apparent to the throne on the box-seat. Straightway, male head-gear is doffed, on all sides, in his honour. These are a workmanlike, useful team of bays, but not showy.

Here comes Sir Henry Oldstead, with his wife beside him, and several relations occupying places behind. A very good-looking team of blacks—his favourite colour—is Sir Henry driving, and the leaders step very well. The policeman, in his anxiety to force members into their right positions in the line of coaches, places his snowy charger in front of the leaders, causing them to swerve and Sir Henry to glance regular broad-swords and pistols, and invoke the reverse of blessings on the over-zealous official's head.

This drag belongs to Sir Alne Kirby. One of the beauties of the season is beside him, and Sir Alne looks highly satisfied with his passengers, his team, and—last, but certainly not least—himself. He is driving four very good-looking black-browns—a handsome team.

Here is a gentleman in a white hat, well known for his hospitality, driving four roans in his coach. On the box beside him is his agreeable wife, who gives some of the pleasantest dances in London, and behind are their numerous olive-branches.

This blue coach belongs to a noble lord who hails from Oxfordshire. Surely, it must be the acme of coachmanship to be able to drive four horses so slowly as he does.

Here is some Jehu, with a large flower in his manly bosom, coming up very late. Who is it? Why, it must be—yes, it certainly is—Dick Wynyard. But he looks not a whit conscious of being extremely late, and comes easily along the drive, as if he were a good quarter of an hour before his time. Lady Lackrent is on the box-seat, intensely nervous and uncomfortable;

but the prospect of a third (perhaps un-
profitable) season with Lady Julia nerves
and induces her to make an effort, and bear
her cross with Spartan fortitude. What a
bevy of beauty has handsome Dick on his
coach! Lady Julia and the two pretty,
fair-haired Miss Mangolds are on the seat
behind him, and opposite the grooms are
sitting Cecil Darnley and—as we live, it is
our old acquaintance, Reggie Burton, looking intensely prim and uncomfortable, and
entirely out of his element—which, in fact,
he is—and is devoutly wishing himself anywhere but on the roof of his cousin's coach.

What a magnificent team Dick is driving!
Very dark chestnuts every one, and hardly
a white speck amongst them. What step-
pers the leaders are! A male hat is doffed
in recognition of Lady Julia, and the off
leader swerves violently, then attempts to
turn round, aided and abetted in this awkward design by his companion. Lady
Lackrent is horribly alarmed, but Dick
promptly, with the utmost coolness and

confidence, thongs the offending quadruped on the nose. The baffled leaders "urge on their wild career," fortunately, in the proper direction, and Lady Lackrent breathes more freely. In "catching" his whip, however, Dick whirls the lash behind his head involuntarily; it coils neatly round the luckless Burton's hat, and rolls that glossy beaver into the dusty road. Dick, full of contrition for his cousin's misfortune, pulls up—utterly oblivious or careless of the fact that he is keeping the rest of the coaches waiting—for the fallen head-gear to be recovered. The ruffled hat is easily smoothed, but Burton's feelings are not so quickly righted. He nearly chokes with suppressed indignation, and vouchsafes not a word in reply to Darnley's mock condolences, or Dick's sincere apology for the mishap.

But the energetic secretary of the club now rushes frantically forward, adjuring Dick to hasten his footsteps (or, rather, his horses' footsteps). That reckless youth

shouts out cheerily in reply, "Very sorry—
watch ten minutes slow."   Then, baring
his silky chestnut head to the prince as he
passes the president's coach, and again to
the royal duchess in her carriage, at the end
of the line, Dick wheels skilfully round
behind the middle line of coaches.

And now they are off at last.   What a
glorious sight it is, to be sure!   Seven and
thirty coaches in line, filing slowly past;
some with horses such as one sees brought
together in no other city in the world.
And then, the sun shining brightly on a
galaxy of beauty and bewildering feminine
toilettes—the former to be surpassed no-
where.   Where else does one ever see the
complexions, the hair, and the fresh *toute
ensemble* of our own fair countrywomen?
Ah, well!   "Nos meilleurs plaisirs sont
ceux que nous n'avons pas," some sarcastic
Gaul has averred.   Dare we confess to being
crusty old bachelors after this quotation,
and affirm that we only covet because we
do not possess?

Dare we hazard the thought that many a cloven hoof and biting tongue is concealed, where we only see bright smiles on tempting, pouting lips, and roses, that come and go like sunbeams, on the peach-like cheeks? Allison says so. But, pooh! we don't believe him a bit; not we. He is cynical and unbelieving where women are concerned. All these fairy-like, charming beings *must* be as good as they look.

What a lovely girl is that in the green barouche over there, and how very animatedly she is talking to the ugly young man on the back seat of her mamma's carriage! *She* never remembers that he has nearly thirty thousand a year, and a place down in the Potteries. Not a bit of it. She only pities him because he is awkward and shy, uncouth and stupid. That lovely form could not hunger for the flesh-pots of Egypt! If Jupiter himself descended on her, in a shower of gold, she would not have him as a lover, like that mercenary Danae did. Not she, indeed! Good, beneficent little Miranda, smile on thy ugly slave Caliban. Verily a modern version of Beauty and the Beast!

The coaches have passed by the statue of grim Achilles—in truth, a goodly array. Some will go down to Alexandra Park, others only so far as the Marble Arch. Let us stroll into the Row, and see the equestrians. Surely "every one" must be abroad to see and be seen on such a lovely morning as this.

We sit down and take out a pennyworth of chair, and the proprietor informs us, as we tender him our coin (as he invariably does every year), that he has never known such a bad season for his chairs before.

What a republic is Rotten Row! and how amusing sometimes! Here Mr. Sarsnett—the draper's assistant who secretly embezzles his employer's money—by paying his penny, may seat himself on a chair next to the mighty Duke of Omnium himself. Flaunting Laïs, Phrynne, and Aspasia, with painted cheeks and belladonna'd eyes, may be grouped around that immaculate spinster, Miss Jane Tractly. And the sporting costermonger, Joe Sprouts, in his sealskin cap with clay pipe stuck in the top, and dirty red handkerchief loosely tied round his dubious-looking neck, may sit down next to the exclusive and gorgeously arrayed Lady Hauton, on his tendering a copper coin for that privilege.

Peer and stockbroker, soldier and Jew, almost jostle one another in the crowded ride. Here is a noble earl, with a huge gardenia in his button-hole, and inimitable glossy hat with curly brim. How does that wondrous tile preserve its constant brilliancy? And what would not that smart member of the Stock Exchange behind him give for the recipe to make his head-covering "beautiful for ever"?

There is a well-known figure on the old white horse with a black cap over its eye. How tightly is that wonderfully stepping animal curbed!

Here, on the big bay, is "Our Sir Jarge,"

as his tenants all call him; and close behind rides the eminent usurer, Mr. Abimelech, on a flashy chestnut.

In the distance, mounted on hog-maned little cobs, come two youths, known respectively to their intimates as "Bijou" and "Tigh." Bijou's loud laugh is heard more than a hundred yards off, following some remark from his companion. His pony certainly is an ugly little animal; but oh, why should he call that otherwise inoffensive quadruped by the uneuphonious name of Rickety Jack?

There, on the roan, is the popular Lady Tyke, as keen about sport in the north as she is about dancing and amusement in general in the south.

Then do we not know, and like well, this charming little lady on the mouse-coloured cob, with her husband on the gallant little grey?

And these two fair sisters, one of whom, doffing his hat, Tigh addresses as "Belinka," with the air of an old friend;

and the other, glancing about, with assumed nonchalance, from the broad back of her pretty little cob Captain?

Here is Lord Loutish, in a pink-striped shirt and red tie, lounging over the rails, with a toothpick in his mouth, by turns yawning fit to dislocate his jaw, and kicking up the gravel with his huge foot.

There goes a youth whom we knew years ago as stout and jovial. He is even stouter now than then; but the joviality and the refreshing, trusting innocence—where are they now? " O tempora! O mores ! " How changed indeed are both ! The once jovial youth has a bad foot, and limps across the Row. " Tigh," in jest, pretends to be about to force his pony to run over his friend, and " Bijou's " loud laugh rings out at the joke and the terror shown by the stout and once jovial youth.

Here is our old friend Alec Drayton, best and most well-informed of comrades, strolling along. As usual, he is in close attendance on a pretty damsel. Where

there is a fair lady, there surely is Alec
Drayton to be found—most devoted of *preux
chevaliers* for a time. Trust him not—the
arch-deceiver!—fair lady. Remember the
song of Balthazar—

> " Sigh no more, ladies, sigh no more ;
> Men were deceivers ever ;
> One foot in sea, and one on shore,
> To one thing constant never."

There are four dark chestnuts, in a well-
appointed drag, being pulled up at the
corner by the clock ; the driver descends,
and then assists a lady down from the box.
From the time she takes to descend, it must
be Lady Lackrent. And so it is that
worldly old lady, who is now walking down
the Row, with Dick Wynyard at her side.

Dick's hat is perpetually in the air, and
he responds, with a pleasant smile, to the
greetings of his numerous acquaintances.
He is thinking in his heart what a bore old
Lady Lackrent is, and secretly wishing that
he could with politeness leave that ancient
peeress to some one else, and go to chat

with one of the fair ladies who have bowed
so smilingly to him. But not a trace of his
inward feelings can be guessed from the expression on his comely face as he turns and
makes some remark to his well-pleased companion.

How was it, though (perhaps Lady Lackrent knew something about it), that Dick
has Lady Julia for a companion, when they
turn and walk back again? He proposes to
sit down; but the young lady, doubtless
pleased with her beau, and perhaps thinking
that his chair may not be next hers if they
do so, declines, on the plea that "exercise
does one so much good, you know, Mr.
Wynyard."

But the clock at the corner points to five
minutes to two, warning Lady Lackrent
that her luncheon hour is very near, and
that she must be hastening homewards.
She invites Dick to partake of that meal
with her in Grosvenor Square, but he pleads
a previous engagement; and Lady Lackrent does not extend her invitation to Cecil

Darnley or Burton, but settles herself in her victoria at the corner with her daughter, and is driven away towards Stanhope Gate.

Need we say that we regret deeply, and are much pained to have to chronicle against Dick's character for strict veracity, that when Lady Lackrent's victoria had driven off, he links his arm in Darnley's, and says, " Come and lunch with me at the club, old fellow, will you ? " And they accordingly mount up on the drag once more, and drive up Piccadilly to the Symposium Club; Darnley laughingly and most appositely quoting, in reference to his companion's " white one " to Lady Lackrent, " I say, Dick, ' O tu splendide mendax !' What a oner you told the old lady just now ! "

CHAPTER XXI.

ANTEROS.

"O love for a year, a week, a day,
But alas! for the love that loves alway."
Sweethearts.

LADY JULIA HERIOT is very unhappy just
now. Six months ago, her shrewd, worldly
mother had striven to impress upon her
daughter the fact that, if anything were
to happen to Lord Lackrent, his widow
and daughter would be in a very different
position, and comparatively poor, as the title
and estates would pass away to a nephew.
Lord Lackrent had a large country place
to keep up, and numerous other calls upon
his purse, which prevented his making any
future provision for his wife other than the

settlements made at his marriage. Therefore, argued the old lady, it behoved her
daughter to make a brilliant match; and
she further reminded her that she had had
two seasons in London already, where, if
she did not lack admirers, she repressed
any warmer feeling than admiration, by her
haughty and chilling manners to possible
suitors for her fair hand.

When they had stayed at High Wynyard, in November last year, Lady Lackrent had settled in her own active mind
that the handsome young owner of that
property would be a very desirable match
for her daughter. Mr. Wynyard came of
a good old family; his estates were in their
own county, and his income must be a
very good one. Lady Lackrent, conning
over all these pros, decided that the alliance would "do" very well, if she could
only bring it about. The shrewd old dame,
however, knew better than to confide her
plans to her imperious daughter, whom she
secretly feared not a little. What more

likely than that that proud young lady might decline to be guided by her loving mamma's worldly counsels, and scornfully reject the proffered alliance if it were ever within her grasp? Lady Lackrent, warned by previous failures, decided in her own mind that it would not further her plans to instruct her daughter in the part she wished her to play, and wisely held her peace on the subject of Dick Wynyard's attractions, spiritual and temporal.

The day before she left High Wynyard, however, the crafty old dame had carefully sounded Lady Nora as to her wishes in respect to her only son. That good lady would, I believe, verily have welcomed a red Comanche squaw, if it would have given Dick pleasure; and as Lady Lackrent adroitly hinted that "Mr. Wynyard seemed to admire my daughter very much," need we say that Lady Nora fell into the trap, and entered heart and soul into the veteran campaigner's plans? She encouraged her son to go over to Appleby; and when the

hunting season was over, and Dick pressed
her, in April, to go to London with him,
Lady Nora would not leave her country
home, but she helped her darling boy to
take a house in Hill Street, and hoped he
"would see a great deal of the Lackrents
in London."

Now, it must not be supposed that Lady
Julia would deliberately set herself to gain
the heart—and fortune—of anybody for
whom she did not care in the least; but
still she was fully alive (as, indeed, what
carefully brought up young lady is not?)
to the advantages of comparative affection
in a large country place, with a deer park
and a house in London to boot, over love
in a cottage, with a maid of all work and
no horses. She had inherited some prac-
tical ideas from her worldly old mamma,
and decided that love in a cottage was
romantic nonsense, and not to be thought
of for one instant. It must indeed have
been edifying to witness the utter amazement, and complete unconcern for his feel-

ings, which this well brought up young lady had evinced, on receiving a proposal from the curate at Appleby, that she should share his heart and worldly goods (the latter comprising a present income of eighty pounds a year).

Just *pour passer le temps*, as she herself had expressed it, she had flirted with poor Mr. Mopes, to lighten the ennui of one dreary winter at Appleby, and affected great interest in the sending out of goloshes and Ulster coats to the benighted natives of Madagascar. This, and other equally beneficent schemes, threw her much into the poor curate's society; and he, poor moth, not having had much experience of the wicked world, or the ways of young ladies, had singed his foolish wings very severely in the light of this brilliant candle.

Lady Julia went up to London soon after receiving this proposal, and speedily forgot the unfortunate curate in a whirl of gaiety. When she returned to Appleby again, she heard that poor Mr. Mopes had gone out as a missionary to Hullabaloo, which every one knows is, of course, one of the South Sea Islands; and it had not troubled her conscience the slightest that she had never heard of him again.

When Lady Julia had stayed at High Wynyard last year, she had liked her host because he was so good-looking and agreeable; and then, there was such an utter absence of conceit in Dick, which took her fancy enormously. Then, he was so expert at all manly exercises; and what woman does not admire a man the more for being able to perform those feats which, by reason of her inferior thews and sinews, she cannot accomplish herself?

Do you really believe that Omphale liked Hercules so well when he wielded the distaff, and. that she would not much rather have watched him performing one of his seven labours—cutting off the many heads of the hydra, for example?

And Helen—although she used to chaff Paris so unmercifully about not going forth to do battle with the Greeks, before the walls of Troy—must have been fully aware, in her own wilful, admiring heart, that the fascinating youth was no coward, else would she have remained with him, after being the wife of stout Menelaus?

If patient Penelope did get a little weary of waiting for mighty Ulysses all those long years, must it not have been a suitor cunning with the bow, or swift of foot in the games, who so nearly induced her to yield? Perhaps he was better at lawn-tennis, or more deadly at potting the long-tails than his rivals, when they were shooting the absent Ulysses' coverts?

It must have been for some reason of this sort. Be sure that deeds of "derring-do" always have appealed, and always will appeal, strongly to a woman's heart.

But *revenons à nos moutons*. Lady Julia had seen a great deal of Dick Wynyard in the course of the winter, and each time she saw him she liked him the more. He was always cheery, attentive, and very good-

natured. She was obliged to acknowledge
to herself, with a pang, that he was all
these to every young lady he spoke to ; but
need we say that, woman-like, she liked
him none the less that they all seemed to
appreciate his attentions, and wilfully shut
her eyes to the fact that he paid no more
attentions to her than to any other well-
favoured young lady?

Lady Julia had fallen desperately in love,
for the first and last time in her life, and
felt unchristian-like feelings kindle in her
breast when any woman—and they were
many—smiled too kindly on handsome
Dick. Medea's love for Jason was nothing
in comparison to the passion that now con-
sumed this once imperious young lady. She
was blind to everything but the fact that
she loved him devotedly and passionately.
Dick was her Alpha and Omega, the beginning and end of her vision. Every time
she parted from him his sunny chestnut
hair and smiling blue eyes haunted her,
making her long passionately for the time

when she should meet him again. Did she now realize that—

> "Alas! the love of woman! it is known
>   To be a lovely and a fearful thing;
> For all of theirs upon that die is thrown,
>   And if 'tis lost, life hath no more to bring."

When these strong, passionate natures once love, it is indeed a fearful thing; and now did she love "not wisely, but too well."

Alas! for the wise precepts of Lady Lackrent, and the worldly maxims that clever dame had so carefully instilled into her daughter's mind. What have they availed her in this crisis? Lady Julia is recklessly, hopelessly in love, and would bid diamonds, horses, position, everything, to take unto themselves wings and fly away; would ask nothing in return, at this moment, but a cottage or a desert island, where she might lie at the feet of the man she adores, and be his humble, loving slave —caring for nothing but his smile, amply repaid for her love by a kindly caress of her ebon locks from his hand, or to be allowed to cover it with burning, passionate kisses.

Oh! how it pains us to have to record such backsliding from the unwritten code, unalterable as the laws of the Medes and Persians of old, Ye shall not marry without a handsome settlement, or carriages, or horses, or a country place, or a title, as the case may be; and on no account permit yourselves to love unsought, or give your love where there is no income or good future prospects. Lady Julia has indeed fallen low from her pedestal! What a warning should she not be to all well brought up young persons, who have ever given their dear mammas the slightest cause for anxiety!

Let us, like Asmodeus, fly off to Grosvenor Square, lift up the roof of No. 100, and look in upon the inmates.

Lady Julia is very sad and silent as she sits at luncheon, and her plate is scarcely touched. The *pâté de foi gras* seems tasteless to-day; the grapes have not the least flavour; and surely M. Framboise has taken to making his cream ices—on which that eminent chef used to pride himself— very insipid now, she thinks.

Lady Lackrent, peering over the flowers in the centre of the table at her handsome daughter, feels almost a pang at her worldly old heart, when she sees her so sad and absent in mind. Twice has Lady Julia returned absurdly irrelevant answers to her remarks; but Lady Lackrent knows of old her daughter's imperious temper, and forbears to comment on the want of appetite and absence of mind that she shows.

Lady Julia looks all the more handsome that she is depressed in spirit. There is a softness in the brilliant dark eyes, and unconsciously a gentle, tender manner almost, which is infinitely more charming in her than the old imperiousness and contradiction.

May we not say—

> " And if we loved her when she won,
> Our love is prouder now "?

"Luncheon seems to take a long time to-day," she says presently, with a sigh. "I think I shall go and lie down, mamma, with a book."

"Very well, my dear; don't forget we have to go to Lady Trotterton's ball to-night; and, Julia!" raising her voice as her daughter goes out into the hall—"will you go to the opera first? Mr. Wynyard has given me his box for to-night, and it will be 'Tannhauser.'"

"Oh no, mamma; I can't bear Wagner's music. You and papa can go alone, and pick me up here afterwards for Lady Trotterton's ball—or take Minna Wurzel with you; she would enjoy the opera."

She knows quite well that Dick Wynyard will not be at the opera, but thinks he may very likely go to Lady Trotterton's. The Mangolds are sure to be there, and a horrible suspicion shoots across her mind, that Dick Wynyard is often very near pretty, fair-haired Nellie Mangold. Semi-ramis, in her wrathful jealousy, could not have looked darker than did Lady Julia's handsome eyes, as this suspicion crosses her mind. She will watch Nellie Mangold's behaviour towards Mr. Wynyard to-night, at Lady Trotterton's, and then if——

She takes up a book—it is one of the popular novels of the day—and reads, with languid interest, that the only care in life of a certain smart member of the *jeunesse dorée* of Paris " was the temperature of his eau-de-Cologne bath ! " She throws down the novel, of which she can read nothing. Dick Wynyard's comely face will appear on every page, and she can think of nothing else.

She looks at the clock, and sees that it is past five. No, she will not go out in the barouche, or to Prince's, this afternoon, she thinks. She will put on her *peignoir*, and have a cup of tea—that always does her good—and then Flounce shall brush her hair. So she rings the bell, and orders the footman to send that experienced Abigail upstairs.

Miss Flounce, returning some twenty minutes later to a heavy tea, with hot buttered toast and unlimited "creases," confides to her especial favourite, Thomas the footman, for whose exuberant calves and carefully trained whiskers she cherishes a profound admiration, that she "can't a-make out her ladyship nohow. Just fancy now, Mr. Tummus," continued Miss Flounce, astonished at such undeserved forbearance on the part of her young mistress, "she ain't a-called me a stoopid fool more nor once in the last fortnit, as I'm a living woman."

"Mr. Tummus" is evidently learned in the ways of women, for he opines that "perhaps her leddyship hev took the complaint wery bad, and wants to be a-keepin' company with a sweetheart, which he don't take to her belike—the which is horful upsettin' to a young woman's feelin's," affirmed "Mr. Tummus," oracularly, insinuating his arm affectionately round Miss Flounce's ample waist.

"Well, I never! The imperence of some folks, indeed!" exclaimed that buxom Abigail, without, however, manifesting the slightest anxiety to disengage herself from "Mr. Tummus's" embrace. "Now, don't, Mr. Tummus; you mustn't. Cook will be a-comin' in."

To which "Mr. Tummus," wise in his generation, and mindful of former favours, replies by a chaste salute, for which "imperence," in spite of her remonstrances, Miss Flounce does not seem so deeply offended after all.

Lady Julia looks radiantly handsome about eleven o'clock, waiting for the carriage to return from the opera. Her dress, of crimson and black, shows off her dark imperial beauty to advantage, and deep red carnations are entwined in her jet black hair.

She takes a last lingering glance at her stately figure reflected in the looking-glass; and wonders if Dick Wynyard will go, after all, to Lady Trotterton's, and what he will think of her toilette.

It only takes ten minutes to get to Bel-
grave Square, and, with the usual happy
knack of servants for misnaming, the
" Countess of Nacklent ! " and " Lady Julia
Heavypot ! " are announced in a stentorian
voice by the major-domo on the staircase,
as they ascend to greet their hostess.

All praise to that great and good woman,
patient as Penelope, untiring as Sybella,
standing at the head of her staircase for
hours to welcome her guests.   How good-
natured she must be to, figuratively, turn
her house out of window for the enjoyment
of others, when, of course, she does not
dance herself, and has no daughters, either,
to enjoy the ball !   Perhaps her " drums "
are very dull, but—" Auctor pretiosa facit."
All honour to her, her balls, at all events,
are of the best in London.

Lady Julia sees at a glance that Dick
Wynyard is not in the room ; but although
she is immediately beset by innumerable
smart young men eager for a valse, she finds
time to notice that Nellie Mangold is already

there, looking exceedingly pretty in some
white gauzy material, with bouquets of
forget-me-nots in her dress and hair, which
suit her fair complexion admirably.

After four dances, without turning her
graceful head, she feels that the man she
loves is standing near her. And so he is.
Reckless Dick has been gambling at the
Symposium, but, taking out a card by accident from amongst a heap of letters, he has
been reminded that Lady Trotterton is "at
home" to him on this evening.

He looks exceedingly handsome, Lady
Julia thinks, as he advances to make his
bow, and affirms that he is "afraid Lady
Julia cannot have a dance to spare for such
a late arrival." Curiously enough, though,
she has a dance to spare, and the very next
valse, too. So she walks off on his arm at
once.

They attempt to float through the crowd,
to the strains of "Geleibt und Veloren,"
but have to stop at the other end of the
room; and Lady Julia, looking up at her

partner with a glance that might have over-
come even St. Anthony, and ever so slightly
pressing his arm almost involuntarily, said,
"Do you remember our first valse at dear
old High Wynyard, Mr. Wynyard?"

"To be sure I do," replied Dick, cheerily;
but, alas! how indifferently, either not no-
ticing or impervious to his partner's glance.
"Rather a different room to this, though,
wasn't it? and not such a crush. Would
you like to try another turn?" And he
is very much surprised to find, at the end
of the dance, that for a young lady so
invariably overburdened with partners, Lady
Julia has an astonishing number of valses
not yet filled up. He engages her for
several, to her great delight; but her joy
is damped the next moment by his taking
her to a seat next Lady Lackrent, and then
leaving her to walk off to speak to Nellie
Mangold.

Lady Julia, somehow, does not enjoy her
ball so much after all. How strange are the
dispositions of Fate! Here is Cecil Darn-

ley, who would give almost anything for a valse with Lady Julia, but cannot prevail on that young lady to grant him anything except "the fourth square from now, Mr. Darnley;" whilst Dick—ungrateful wretch! —if he could do so consistently with politeness, would make over all his valses with the wayward beauty to his friend with the utmost pleasure and sang-froid. And so it will be, perhaps, to the end of time. When the New Zealander dances on the ruins of London Bridge, there will be surely some such crumpled rose-leaf to disturb his peace of mind.

Dick comes up for a last word as Lady Julia is taking her departure. "Don't forget that you dine with me on Saturday, at Hurlingham."

"Oh no, Mr. Wynyard! Who are the party?"

"Sir Henry Oldstead, yourselves, Mr. Darnley, Ralph Allison, Mr. Clitheroe, Moller, and—let me think—oh yes! the Mangolds, of course."

CHAPTER XXII.

AT HURLINGHAM.

"Come into my parlour,
Said the spider to the fly."

DICK WYNYARD is sitting alone in the break-
fast-room of his house in Hill Street; a pile
of unopened letters, of most of which he
guesses the purport, lie beside his plate,
and he holds a long meerschaum pipe by its
amber mouthpiece between his teeth.

Dick is beginning to find that the meta-
phorical shoe pinches him very sharply.
Twelve thousand a year is a very good income, no doubt; but when five thousand of
that, at least, has to be spent on a large
estate, with a big country place, a town
house, a stud of hunters, and a string of

racehorses to keep up—not to mention a
bijou establishment in the north-west dis-
trict of London for Mdlle. Coralie, the
famous danseuse, a highly expensive luxury
—and unlimited play, night after night, at
the Symposium Club, money quickly takes
unto itself wings, and vanishes.

Open-hearted, generous Dick's purse was
always at the service of his needy friends,
and many were the "few hundreds" lent to
(and, of course, never returned by) his impecunious acquaintances by that reckless
youth. He had not the slightest idea of
the value of money, and with him, to see a
thing and covet it was to possess, if it could
be bought. A horse, a picture, an organ
which played dance music like a full regi-
mental band, and cost him over £900—it
was all the same to reckless Dick; whatever took his fancy, that did he surely
become the possessor of, utterly regardless
of cost.

We have never seen him so grave, since
poor Horace Audley's death, as he looks

this morning. There are already a few lines on the comely young face which surely have no right to be there as yet, and there are dark rings under the usually smiling blue eyes. The mouth, rather a wide one, and his worst feature, is almost concealed by a long silky, golden-brown, almost auburn moustache, which he is now biting restlessly, and twisting about with his long slim fingers.

Pull up, Dick, while there is yet time. Sell your racehorses, and give up your town house; don't see so much of your so-called "friends;" abandon Mdlle. Coralie, the danseuse, to some one else's care, and shun the card-room of the Symposium.

But not the slightest idea of putting down any of his expenses crosses his mind, and he is only thinking how he can raise more money. Sir Henry Oldstead has warned him that his income will not stand the repeated calls upon it; but that prince of good fellows has no idea of the frightful losses, at play, of his young friend, or that he had not only spent all the ready money left by his grandfather, but more than the year's income, and dipped deeply into his capital.

Yes, it must be done, Dick thinks; and, ringing the bell, he orders the brougham to come round in twenty minutes, and proceeds, with the aid of his valet, to take off his velvet smoking-suit and induct himself into outdoor apparel.

This operation being completed to his satisfaction, he puts an exotic in his buttonhole, lights a huge cigar, and slowly descends the staircase, humming an air from "La Perichole," drawing on a pair of pale primrose-coloured gloves, and fastening the two buttons at each wrist with great care.

When he reaches the foot of the staircase, however, he calls out to his valet, "Tirer, tell Ortolan we shall be twelve at luncheon to-day, and order the drag to come round at three o'clock. I am going down to Hurlingham, and shall dine there."

The brougham door is shut with a bang,

and he is driven rapidly to a dingy-looking house in a small street off the Strand. Dick jumps out and rings the bell loudly. Truly, over this doorway should be written in large characters—

"Abandon hope, all ye who enter here."

It is the abode of that eminent usurer, Mr. Samuel Arachney.

"Yes, Mr. Arachney is at home, and disengaged," he is informed by a servant, who, so far as outward appearances go, might have been easily mistaken. for a high dignitary of the Church, so respectable and imposing was his manner; and Dick is ushered into a handsomely furnished room with numerous oil paintings hung on the walls, each picture having a label inscribed with the name of some celebrated artist, ancient or modern.

Mr. Arachney is there, apparently engaged in perusing the *Times*. To look at him in the street, you would hesitate whether to put him down as a sporting

parson of the old school, or to mistake him
for a certain distinguished chairman of com-
mittees in the Upper House. His broad-
brimmed hat, with beaver underneath, is
the very essence of respectability; he is
always dressed in black, and sports a swal-
low-tail coat and high waistcoat, morning
and evening; his broad black cravat is
wound three times round a scrupulously
clean, stiffly starched high collar; he affects
a bland, benevolent smile, and has never
been known to give a copper in secret
charity in his life; yet his name figures
occasionally in his parish lists of subscrip-
tions for the sending out of chignons and
lace petticoats to Zanzibar, or black silk
stockings and patent-leather dancing-pumps
for the depraved and dusky Hottentot; and
no doubt he is a pious and energetic churchwarden, a pillar of the Church, and a shining
light (probably not hid under a bushel) at
Clapham, where he has a handsome villa,
and a Mrs. and a dozen little Arachneys,
for aught we know.

He rises as Dick enters, bending his bald head with an unctuous smile, rubbing his hands slowly with invisible soap, and blandly inquires what he can " do for Mr. Wynyard this lovely morning." He is " sorry to see that Consols are down; and money is very tight just now in the City—yes, ve-e-ry tight, unfortunately," affirmed Mr. Arachney, pursing up his lips, buttoning up his trouser-pockets, and from habit (which, they say, is second nature) turning up his eyes sanctimoniously to the ceiling.

No need to ask what he can do for Dick Wynyard. He knows very well, and everything about that reckless youth—his position, estates, present income, and future prospects.

Ye gods! what do these men (bloodsuckers some) not know? " Come into my parlour, said the spider to the fly." Poor foolish, misguided fly, when will you get out again? Once that indefatigable insect has drawn you into his web, he will not abandon you, probably, until every leg has been crunched up in his voracious maw, every drop of your blood run dry.

Dick's business is soon arranged, and by a few strokes of a pen he is accommodated —at an exorbitant interest—with the sinews of war in the shape of a large cheque. He resists the offer of taking part of the sum out in dubious oil paintings, affirms that he "don't want and won't have" some very "curious" old "dry sherry," or "two cases of cigars imported direct from Cuba," and prepares to take his leave of Mr. Samuel Arachney.

"Ah, now, you are too hard on me, Mr. Wynyard," said that eminent Christian usurer. "You are, indeed! It's almost like giving money away. Well, well, you talk me over just as easy as your poor father did. I do believe Captain Wynyard would have persuaded a fox out of his earth," affirmed Mr. Arachney, jocosely, waving at an imaginary fox with his heavy gold eye-glasses. "Pardon the liberty, Mr. Wynyard, but he was called 'Blarney Dick' in his regiment; and well he might be—ha! ha! ha! You must be going? Well, good morning, Mr. Wynyard—go-o-od morning," bowing, and washing his hands with the invisible soap again. "You had better take some of that dry sherry; you had, really now. Well, if you won't—— "

Dick jumps into his brougham, conscious that he has promised to pay an exorbitant interest for the large sum that he has just borrowed. But what does he care? It will be a long time before he will be called upon to pay; and then he can always renew, he thinks. · So, who more gay and debonair at luncheon than he, when entertaining a party of ten?—rattling away cheerily, as if he had not a single care in the world—as if he had not signed away more than a year's income that very morning.

The drag comes round to Hill Street punctually at three. Dick and his friends stand at the window, watching the handsome dark chestnuts champing their bits, tossing their heads, and pawing the ground with their hoofs, impatient of delay. Mr. Bantam, the head coachman, is sitting on the box, holding the reins, immovable and impassive as the marble Memnon, anon dexterously flicking his horses to make them stand out and show themselves—not a muscle of his face moving as he hears his charges appraised, by admiring by-standers, at prices ranging from two to six hundred each.

Dick drives a party of men down to Hurlingham on the drag, and as he skilfully wheels his coach alongside a few others, Darnley catches sight of Lady Lackrent's barouche coming on to the polo ground from the opposite direction.

Cecil Darnley is very smartly dressed—his boots are resplendent with varnish, his nether garments unexceptionable, the pearl-grey gloves faultless—and yet, why does he feel that his hat is too tight, his shining boots too large, and think that his continu-ations hang badly? And why, when a few moments before he had been lively and gay, should his tongue feel dry, his throat parched, and his usual *aplomb* completely desert him, as he advances to meet Lady Julia, and drops his walking-stick in shaking hands with that handsome young lady? Moreover, he finds that he has nothing more novel to say than "What a fine day it is!" and hopes "that Lady Julia is quite well."

Alas! alas! what fools does the wicked, naked little god make of men and women; shooting his arrows at young and old, rich and poor, respecting neither sex nor age.

Lady Julia is "quite well, thank you," and smiles sweetly at Darnley's discomfiture, either ignorant or heedless of the cause. She accepts a chair from him, and sits down under a sheltering umbrella-tent to watch the game of polo, which is being carried on with considerable vigour; the match being between four of the Guards, and the same number of the Hurlingham Club.

Presently Dick and Darnley go off to

the pigeon-shooting, and their attention is speedily engrossed by that exciting sport. Miss Mangold and Lady Julia, tired of watching the polo, go, half an hour later, to take a stroll through the pretty Hurlingham gardens together, and admire the beautiful salmon-coloured double carnations in the conservatory; then they turn in at the open door leading to the pigeon-shooting ground.

"Oh! I do think pigeon-shooting is so cruel," said soft-hearted little Nellie Mangold. "I hardly like to go and look on at it."

"What nonsense!" exclaimed her companion rather sharply. "The pigeons don't know they are going to be shot any more than partridges or pheasants do. Besides, pheasants are sometimes nearly as tame as chickens; and when papa shoots the coverts at Appleby, they have sometimes to be almost kicked up before they will rise."

"Oh, Julia, but then——"

"They kill thousands of nearly tame

pheasants in a battue, I tell you, and yet no one calls that cruel."

Dick and Darnley are the last two left in a sweepstake, and are shooting off the tie.

Both have been shooting in good form to-day, and have killed nine birds in succession. Darnley is just about to cry " Pull ! " to the trapper, and shoot, when he catches sight of Lady Julia's dress, and burns to distinguish himself before his fair ladye-love.

Need we say that that fortunate blue-rock flies off scathless, and perches itself ex-ultingly on the top branch of a tree in the garden ?

Still, Dick may yet miss too. Not a bit of it. He lays down his cigar in the tin, takes a sight at every trap in succession with the utmost coolness, and crying out " Pull ! " grasses his pigeon scientifically with the first barrel, thus winning the sweepstakes.

Then they migrate to the pleasant lawn for tea, where the Guards band discourses sweet music.

After tea they while away the time until dinner by playing lawn-tennis, and—as Lady Julia would insist on playing on Darnley's side, to his delight, and with most unaccountable perversity, considering that she would have dearly liked to be Dick's partner (both for lawn-tennis and for life)— she sustained a defeat at the hands of that skilful youth and Nellie Mangold.

Dick had secured a table by the window in the dining-room, and—the extravagant fellow!—had engaged the services of the Hungarian band, who take up their quarters in the conservatory, and play admirably during dinner time.

Lady Lackrent is enjoying herself very much this evening. Seated at the end of the table, opposite her host, that excellent old lady pronounces the cooking "very fair," the whitebait "fresh," the champagne "really extremely good, and iced *à merveille.*" Altogether, she is well pleased with everything, but is somewhat discomposed by her host saying suddenly, "I asked

Moller—that American you met at High Wynyard—to dine with us to-night" (Lady Lackrent visibly shudders), "but he is going across the Atlantic on Tuesday, and wouldn't come."

Lady Lackrent is immensely relieved, and mendaciously replies—

"Oh, I am so sorry. He *was* so agreeable, and *so* original. Such quaint stories he used to tell, too!"

We regret to state that, on hearing this assertion, Allison furtively kicks Darnley under the table, nearly causing that gallant young sabreur to choke with suppressed chuckles.

"Try some of that suprême de canard, won't you, Clitheroe?" said Dick to a young Foreign Office clerk; "it is excellent."

"Àpropos of ducks," said Allison, "I never eat one now without being reminded of an amusing anecdote. I think it was one of Dean Ramsay's Scotch stories. A Scotch baillie," continued he, "was once summoned before a committee of the House of Lords to give evidence about fixing a close time for wild-fowl; and the Duke of Newcastle, as president, asked him, amongst other questions, what sized shot he used for certain birds. 'Eh! jest the saäme as for dukes an' sich wild fules,' replied the old baillie; and he was astonished to witness the anger which his reply called up on the noble president's countenance. He persisted in his assertion, however; and things might have gone badly for the old baillie, but that a Scotch peer explained that the worthy man intended no disrespect, and meant, in fact, to say that he used the shot 'for ducks and such wild-fowl.'"

" Capital!" exclaimed Darnley, opening his lips for nearly the first time. "The duke's face must have been a picture. What a fellow you are for telling stories, Allison! You're always at it. Isn't he, Lady Julia?"

That young lady smiles faintly. She does not like Allison very much, for she knows his cynical opinion of women; besides, she has an impression that he has been sarcastic more than once at her expense, and feels that her fascinations are as wasted on him as the splashing waves beating against a grim rock. What fair lady would not disapprove of such astounding insensibility?

After dinner all go out on the lawn for coffee, and the male cigar is not tabooed. Lady Julia feels strangely happy. After all, Dick (she loves to call him "Dick" in her own mind) has not paid very much attention to that minx, Nellie Mangold, at dinner, and now the man she loves is walking by her side.

She is not usually very romantic, but the still night, the cool breeze wafting the scent of the lime trees, the soft moonlight, and Dick's low, pleasant voice, all conspire to make her fancy herself almost in a delicious dream. She thinks—

> "And if this be but a dream,
> Then let me never wake again."

Cecil Darnley feels utterly out of sorts, and hipped. Like Sisyphus, when that wearisome stone would roll down the hill every time he so nearly reached the top, Darnley feels that no sooner does he think that he has mounted in Lady Julia's good graces, than something happens to make him aware that he is as far from his goal as ever. He is dejected and out of spirits, because his friend is walking with his (Darnley's) idol, and is so absent in his replies to Lady Lackrent, that she sets him down in her mind as one of the most idiotic young guardsmen she has ever had the misfortune of meeting.

Poor Darnley cannot endure her vivacious chatter, so, rushing away from the party, he luckily finds a hansom-cab, buries himself and his sorrows in it, and goes back to London without saying good night to any one.

Lady Lackrent, of course, occupies the box-seat of the drag going back to town, and asks her charioteer if he will dine with them in Grosvenor Square the following week.

"Very sorry, but I can't," replied Dick. "I have taken a cottage near Epsom for the races, and shall be down there all next week.'

"Have you a horse in the Derby, Mr. Wynyard ? "

"Yes.   I bought a horse, called Dædalus, from Mr. Sinnington.   No chance of winning, I'm afraid, but I have backed him for a place."

"I hope you may have good luck," said Lady Lackrent, blandly. "Of course you mean to go to Ascot this year ? "

"Oh, certainly!   A horse of mine, called Undine, is running for the cup, you know," replied Dick ; "and I have taken a cottage near Windsor for the week, and mean to send the drag down."

"Charming !" said Lady Lackrent.

"Yes, it will be very nice.   Will you and your daughter come and stay with me for the races down there ?   I have asked Sir John Mangold and his daughters already."

Lady Lackrent secretly decides that Dick

must be very much *épris* of her handsome
daughter, and avers, with considerable truth,
that she is "delighted to accept" for herself
and daughter, but that " my husband does
not care for racing, and will not ever go;"
an announcement that does not seem to
cause Dick any very great anguish.

He drives all the party to their respective
abodes, and then changes his clothes in
Hill Street. Half an hour later, we regret
to have to chronicle, he is seated in a
hansom, on his way to play at the Symposium
Club.

CHAPTER XXIII.

THE MAJESTY OF THE LAW.

"I know you lawyers can with ease
   Twist words and meanings as you please;
That language, by your skill made pliant,
   Will bend to favour every client."

GAY.

"DEAR me! why, I had very nearly left my wig and gown behind," exclaims a barrister, stowing away those paraphernalia of the law in a capacious portmanteau; "that would have been awkward."

The speaker is no other than our old acquaintance, Reginald Burton, now blossomed into the full-blown advocate. He took a very creditable degree from Bruce College, Oxford, has eaten his dinners with much satisfaction to himself, and doubtless much profit to his country, and some time ago was called to the bar, since which he has been already honoured with several briefs from admiring clients in consequence of the painstaking, industrious way he conducted his first case.

To-day he is even more solemn than usual, for do not the Dullchester assizes begin to-morrow; and has he not been selected to serve as junior counsel under that famous and crafty advocate, Mr. Wheedler, Q.C., in the breach of promise case of Doveton *versus* Swainly?

Burton feels that the eyes of his country will be upon him to-morrow, and has worked up his case with praiseworthy industry. Indeed, he is not quite certain in his own mind that he could not advocate the claims of injured innocence almost as ably and satisfactorily as that famous man, Mr. Wheedler, Q.C., himself. Burton is never likely to suffer from over-diffidence, and has a most profound opinion of his own abilities.

Burton is whirled by the early express down to the old cathedral. city of Dull-chester. That ordinarily intensely dull, virtuous city has brightened up at the prospect of the assizes; balls and concerts, public dinners and theatricals, are to be the order of the day—or rather of the night—whilst criminals are waiting in their cells to be sentenced to death or imprisonment, as the case may warrant, by that stern judge and terror of malefactors, Mr. Justice Minos.

As the train draws up at the Dullchester station, a flourish of trumpets is heard, and the High Sheriff of Drearyshire, attended by his chaplain, and three gigantic footmen in gorgeous livery, with three-cornered silver-laced hats and silk stockings, comes forward to meet the judge, conducts him to his old yellow family coach which is in waiting, and they drive off to the Town Hall.

Here the charge is read. " My Lord, the Queen's Justice," is duly sworn in, and then he is driven by the High Sheriff to the judge's lodgings outside the town.

The High Sheriff gave a dinner to the
bar that evening at his hotel, followed by
a ball, at which most of the beauty and
fashion of Drearyshire are present, and the
fun is fast and furious for every one in Dullchester except the poor criminals waiting
in their cells for trial.

The next morning, amidst a flourish of
trumpets, the High Sheriff drove off to the
judge's lodgings, and conducted that stern
official to the Town Hall, where, silence
having been proclaimed, Mr. Justice Minos
delivered his charge to the grand jury.

He comments on the very unsatisfactory
character of the assize list, and delivers a
long speech.

Then the ordinary business of the assize
is proceeded with, and sundry malefactors
summarily convicted and sentenced in the
Crown Court.

A peculiar case is next on the list.

Mr. Justice Minos, to their great disgust
and annoyance, has most peremptorily refused to allow any ladies to sit on the

bench, and now he gives the order to clear the court of all women whilst the present case is being heard.

Great dissatisfaction on the part of the " ladies," and some endeavour to shrink out of sight of the usher, and remain to hear the full details of a highly flavoured case.

The usher turns out all he can see, and then Mr. Justice Minos observed sarcastic- ally, in a loud voice, " Proceed with this case now, Mr. Trouncer.   All *honest* women have left the court."

At least a score of " ladies " shrink guiltily away out of court at this speech. Then the case goes on.

At last (what an age it has seemed to Burton!) the important case of Doveton *versus* Swainly is next on the list in the Nisi Prius Court.   Every one is on the *qui vive*.   All the pigtails of the listless barris- ters wag with excitement, and some draw out sheets of notepaper to make caricatures of the suitors.   Even the judge smiles a little permissively, and every one prepares for much fun and laughter—every one, that is, with the exception of the unhappy defendant, who will not see the point of the jokes at all, and is likely to have a very uncomfortable time of it, writhing under the bullying cross-examination of Mr. Wheedler, Q.C.

"Now, then, who's in this case?"

"I am for the plaintiff, my lud," says Mr. Wheedler, jumping up, "with my learned friend, Mr. Burton."

"I am retained for the defence, my lud," said Mr. Wagg, "with my learned friend and leader, Mr. Serjeant Caustic."

Then the case proceeds. Mr. Wheedler delivers his charge (as he says) "as briefly as possible."

"Gentlemen of the jury," began Mr. Wheedler, "I shall occupy as little of your valuable time as possible" (a grin). "These cases are frequently of a very serious nature, and I can rely on you, gentlemen, after the sagacity you have shown to-day, to judge of this case like the men of the world you seem to be." (Here the twelve stolid farmers rouse themselves, visibly interested by the subtle flattery, and crane their bucolic necks to listen more attentively to the voice of the charmer.)

"The circumstances of the case, gentlemen, are of a peculiarly harrowing nature. It seems that my hapless client—twice a widow already, gentlemen—met the defendant at a small tea-party, and, having a warm, impressionable heart, fell a too easy victim to the fascinations of this bucolic Adonis. He accompanied my client home, visited her frequently, and—and remained to tea! And I shall presently bring evidence to show that not only did he put his arm round her waist, and embrace her"—(here Mr. Wheedler was visibly affected)—"yes, embrace her, gentlemen—but I hope to convince you clearly that he made her an offer of marriage, which she as surely accepted.

"Well, gentlemen, things went on as things generally do in these cases. The defendant's motto was apparently, 'Wein, weib, und gesang,' for he continued to profess the warmest affection for my too confiding client—drank tea, and sang songs with her; but, uniting the wiliness of the serpent with the softness of the dove, gentlemen, he craftily only made her verbal assurances of love—and marriage—and never penned any of those tender effusions breathing love—and marriage—which might have been expected of him.

"Finally, gentlemen, after several months of this sort of philandering, my unfortunate client began to suspect that the defendant's intentions were something akin to those of Harcourt's to the Irish lady—'strictly *dishonourable*;' and on her pressing him to carry out his promise of marrying her, he is reported to have denied ever having offered marriage, and absolutely refused to have anything whatever to do with the widow Doveton.

"My unfortunate client," continued Mr. Wheedler, pathetically, "had no other resource left but to bring this action; and, actuated by purely disinterested motives, and legal advice, has requested damages which I feel certain you will not consider excessive, when I say that they are only laid at the very moderate sum of five thousand pounds."

An "Ah—h—h!" runs through the court, sternly repressed by the usher bawling out, " Silence ! "

"I now leave the case in your hands, gentlemen of the jury," said Mr. Wheedler, persuasively, "confident that full justice will be meted out to my fair client, and will call some witnesses. Call John Hodge," he continued, reading from a paper in his hand.

A stolid-looking rustic is pushed into the witness-box, grinning vacantly at the crowd.

" Now," said Mr. Wheedler, " your name is John Hodge, I believe, and you are a native of the hamlet of Little Sucklington ? Answer me, please."

" Ees, oi be," replied the yokel, on the

broad grin at the astounding knowledge shown of his private affairs.

"Now, just be kind enough to collect your thoughts, and tell the jury as briefly as possible all you know of this sad case."

"Well, Muster Swainly ar hired me, ar did, last Martinmas hirings."

"Kindly confine yourself to the case, please, Mr. Hodge."

"Well, sez oi to Jim Mugsby——"

"Never mind Jim Mugsby."

"Whoy, then," said Mr. Hodge, desperately, "oi thought as how Farmer Swainly was a-coortin o' Widder Doveton."

"Why did you think so?" inquired Mr. Wheedler, blandly.

"Cos ar puts un arm aroond ar waist one moonlit night arter a tea-drinkin' ar mind well. 'Oh, ma loove, you is as bootiful as a star, you is,' sez he, 'an' a sight handsomer nor my prize Berkshire sow!'"

Roars of laughter from the crowd in

court, promptly suppressed, however, by the judge.

"Well," said Mr. Wheedler, triumph- antly, "and after he had compared her to his pet Berkshire sow, what did he do?"

"Whoy, er joost put un arm aroond er waist ag'in, and give un a buss. Sich a smack as it were!" said Mr. Hodge, re- flectively.

Loud laughter in the court.

"A 'buss' is a kiss, I suppose?"

"Ees, it be—you knows that well enoof, yer do." (Laughter.)

"Thank you, Mr. Hodge. That will do. Stand down."

"Wait a little," said Mr. Serjeant Caustic; "I should like to ask the witness a few questions. Now, listen to me," continued Serjeant Caustic, shaking his forefinger impressively at the witness. "What age is your master, Mr. Swainly?"

"Whoy, thirty-one, in coorse."

"Ah, 'thirty-one, in coorse.' And pray

what age do you suppose the widow Doveton to be?"

"Whoy, arl a parish know she be a-turned
a forty an' more."

"Indeed! And she has buried two husbands already, has she not? Now, remember you are on your oath, John Hodge;
so take care."

"What d'ye go a-badgering a chap for
now?" inquired Mr. Hodge, irascibly. "In
coorse every one knows she's a-buried two
hubbies—and a precious good job for them
hubbies, too," he added, provoking a roar
of laughter, and a smile from even the stern
Mr. Justice Minos.

"Thank you. That will do, Mr. Hodge,"
said Serjeant Caustic, cheerfully. "Stand
down."

The rest of the witnesses were mostly of
this type. Mr. Wheedler, Q.C., was bland-
ness itself, so tender was he in delicately
examining the witnesses. Mr. Serjeant
Caustic, on the other hand, endeavoured to
browbeat them in his cross-examination in

every possible way, forcing them to con-
tradict themselves—irritating some, nearly
frightening others out of the few senses
they possessed.

Mr. Wheedler is rising to make his speech
for the plaintiff, when suddenly he puts his
hand to his head, turns very pale, and sits
down abruptly. Then he says faintly, "My
lud, I am seized with vertigo. I am subject
to these fits. I *must* retire from court, and
—and leave the case in the hands of my—
learned junior, Mr. Burton."

Mr. Serjeant Caustic smiles triumphantly.
Now, indeed, is victory within his grasp.
With Mr. Wheedler *hors de combat*, his
junior is sure to make a mess of the case,
the serjeant thinks.

A wicked young barrister whispers to
Burton, " By Jove, Starchy, I wouldn't be
in your shoes now for something ! "

Burton's feelings are mixed, however.
He has a few misgivings, but he reflects
that Fortune is favouring him most unex-
pectedly, and that now is the time to strike

out boldly for himself, and make a mark.
He has got up all the points of the case
carefully. After all, he *can* speak, he
thinks, and hurriedly ransacks his memory
for all the classical quotations he can
think of, wherewith to bewilder the stolid-
looking jury.

He rises up boldly, and, clearing his throat,
twice says, "Gentlemen of the jury. My unhappy client needs your sympathy more than
ever now; for she has lost the services of
that able advocate, my learned friend Mr.
Wheedler, and has to look for support from
a comparatively feeble reed, in the shape of
her junior counsel—myself."

Burton does not really think so in the
least, and is further emboldened by the behaviour of the jury, who wag their heads
patronizingly and benignly, thereby silently
intimating that they will bestow their
valuable attention upon him in spite of his
youth and presumed inexperience.

Burton proceeds :—

" My fair client, gentlemen, met the

defendant first, we have proved, at a small tea-party. Over the sociable muffin, the seductive crumpet, and the invigorating bohea, a friendship was formed, which soon ripened into a warmer feeling—into love. Yes, gentlemen, into love!" said Burton, warming with his subject.

"It has been proved," he continued, "that the defendant had on a red tie and green kid gloves when he first met my fair client. Now, I ask you, gentlemen of the jury, as men of the world, could a fond, foolish woman resist these adornments when coupled with the fatal fascinations of the defendant"—(the defendant was hideous as Polyphemus)—"I say, could she be expected to shut her eyes to the attractions of this agricultural Lothario, when adorned with the adventitious aids of a red tie and green kid gloves?

"We know that women are weak and vain," declared Burton, eloquently. "How could my client resist the soft impeachment of being compared to this man's pet Berk-

shire sow? No, gentlemen!" striking his
hand on his own knee. "This was a subtle
Machiavellian piece of flattery that no impressionable woman could be expected to
resist. It was worthy of the great Talley-
rand himself. And then, as well as this,
a witness has declared that he followed up
his flattering speech by putting his arm
round the widow Doveton's waist!

"Now, gentlemen," continued Burton,
impressively, "my learned friend Mr. Serjeant Caustic may perhaps try to make a
point out of the fact that my client is ten
years older than the defendant, and is,
moreover, a widow for the second time—
perhaps he will even say that widows are
proverbially dangerous—but I will ask you,
gentlemen of the jury, to dismiss these
points of evidence from your minds altogether!

"Is the age of chivalry gone by?" he
asked excitedly, sawing his arm in the air.
"Was the time of the Golden Age better
than the present? Should we have to say—

'Quam bene Saturno vivebant rege priusquam
Tellus in longas est patefacta vias'?

No, gentlemen! Perish the thought that a fond, foolish woman should be deceived, merely because she is older in years than her lover!

"Well, gentlemen, acquaintance ripened into friendship, friendship into love, and before many months they were most deeply attached to one another. Pyramus and Thisbe, Acis and Galatea, Cupid and Psyche, Hero and Leander could not have been more devoted than this loving couple. Indeed, the defendant might not inaptly be compared to Leander, inasmuch as he had tumbled head foremost into a duck-pond, one dark night, when he was going to visit his devoted Hero—my fair client."

Laughter in the court, and Burton pauses a moment for breath.

"And now, gentlemen," he continued, pathetically, "I come to a heart-rending point of the sad story. Imagine the feelings of the hapless Queen Dido when

Æneas forsook her, of Cleopatra when she heard that Antony had rejoined Octavia. Think of the agonizing feelings of Ariadne, deserted by the heartless and perfidious Theseus, left weeping on the sandy shore. Try to imagine the anguish of Andromache when she saw the body of ill-fated Hector dragged round the walls of Troy by cruel Achilles. Picture to yourselves the tears of Niobe at her misfortunes, the cruel sufferings of Tantalus when the cup was at his lips, and the luscious fruit escaped from him, and you have some slight idea of the agonizing feelings of my too confiding, unhappy client. This man had breathed honeyed words into her ear—words which, may we not say—

'Hæc olim meminisse juvabat'?

And then, after so short a time—for no reason that has been shown, gentlemen—he chose to change his mind. Alas!

'Quantum mutatus ab illo Achille qui——'

"But I won't continue, gentlemen," said Burton, with praiseworthy emotion. "You have heard the evidence of the defendant's heartlessness—you have heard the details of his infamous, shameless abandonment of my fair client after breathing words of love into her, alas! too willing ears; and I appeal to you, gentlemen of the jury, to know what my unfortunate client could do but seek that redress in a court of justice which is denied her so basely elsewhere!

"The damages, gentlemen of the jury" (very persuasive was Burton at this point) "are fixed at the very moderate sum of five thousand pounds—a small salve, gentlemen, for a deeply wounded — almost broken — heart; and I will terminate my address by thanking you for the patience with which you have listened to me, and sit down, assured that you will find a verdict in favour of the plaintiff, my client.

"Let me end with the lines of the Greek poet whom you all know, gentlemen—

$$\text{'}\pi\lambda\epsilon\alpha\sigma\epsilon\tau\iota\pi\upsilon s\ \kappa o\iota\nu\ \dot{\omega}\ \theta\dot{\eta}\rho\epsilon\alpha\lambda\mu$$
$$\mu\dot{\eta}\kappa\lambda\bar{\iota}\bar{\epsilon}\nu\tau'\ \iota\xi\theta\dot{\eta}\ \gamma\alpha\lambda\tau\omega\beta\alpha\kappa\ \sigma\iota\rho\sigma\nu o\upsilon.\text{'}\text{"}$$

Considerable   applause   (sternly   and

promptly ·repressed) followed Burton's speech as he sat down, feeling that he had acquitted himself miraculously.

The barrister sitting next to him at the table said, "Bravo, old Starchy! I never expected you to humbug them all half as well as you did."

Mr. Serjeant Caustic rose to reply, and paid a tribute to his "learned young friend's very able speech." But in vain did he point out to the jury that the widow was a designing woman, ten years older than his foolish client, who had been, in fact, completely entrapped. "She has buried two husbands already," averred Serjeant Caustic. "Who knows," he demanded, with startling audacity, "that she has not a third alive somewhere?"

In vain was he sarcastic and bitter about the wiles of women, and of widows especially. In vain did he enlarge on the enormity of the damages claimed, and ridicule the idea of money being a salve for a woman's heart. He thumped, and rode

this Pegasus nearly to death. With wither-
ing sarcasm the eloquent serjeant ridiculed
"a heart that could beat so slowly and
calculatingly. A heart," he continued,
thumping despairingly on the table, "that
could have been compared to the torpid,
sluggish feelings of a Berkshire sow! Troy
was taken by treachery," he averred. "This
Delilah had cut off Samson's hair when he
was asleep, and entrapped the luckless defendant under false pretences!"

In vain was all his eloquence, appealing
or sarcastic. The jury refused to listen to
the voice of the charmer, charm he never
so wisely; and when they left the box after
the judge's speech to go into their room to
consult, every one felt that the verdict was
a foregone conclusion.

The court became a perfect Babel when
the jury were out of the box, and the
judge had retired to his own room. In
vain did the usher indignantly endeavour
to prevent men from putting on their hats.
The sitting had been long, the excitement

intense, and they must relieve their pent-up feelings.

The jury have been away for a long time —more than half an hour. Surely there cannot be any disagreement after the plain way in which the judge in his summing up almost commanded them to find a verdict for the plaintiff?

Come with us, dear reader, and we will fly with you through the keyhole of the jury's room, and look what these bucolic Solons are about.

They are disputing about the amount of damages, and one obstinate juror holds out for no compensation whatever for the widow Doveton's presumedly broken heart. He argues that she was quite old enough to take care of herself, and refuses pertinaciously to give in, although the dinner hour is fast approaching.

"Ar tell ye what it is, Jacob," at last said the enraged foreman, hungry and imperious; "if ye don't give in at wunst, we'll git nor a bite nor a soop o' dinner through yer contrariness, and—and ar'll tak' away ma coostom from ye, too, ar will. So theer, now!'"

Mr. Jacob is terrified. The foreman is a well-to-do grazier, and Jacob is a somewhat impecunious butcher—moreover, deeply indebted to him already; so he abandons any wild ideas about justice that he may entertain, and gives in his adhesion to his brother jurors.

They go back into court; the judge is recalled, and not a sound is heard but the foreman's voice, as he declares a unanimous verdict for the plaintiff—"Damages, two thousand two hundred pounds."

Burton had made his mark. That clever young gentleman had noticed the headings of Mr. Wheedler's speech, already noted down and hidden under the leaves of his blotting-paper. Each time he had looked pathetically at the stolid jurymen, and then down at the table, he had culled ideas from the headings of the eminent Q.C.'s speech, which may partly account, perhaps, for the eloquence which so electrified his brother barristers and the clouded brains of the Dullchester jury.

END OF VOL. I.

PRINTED AT THE CAXTON PRESS, BECCLES.

Lightning Source UK Ltd.
Milton Keynes UK
UKHW030821191120
373623UK00014B/191